A Killer Within:

DOWN BUT NOT OUT

by

Sarah Ferguson

Vincella,
"... He is a rewarder
of those that diligently
seek Him.
Hebrews 11:6
Sarah Ferguson.
10/14/15

1

Acknowledgments

In appreciation to:

Dr. Sezilee Reid for reading the beginning concept.

Dr. Brenda Cromwell for carefully and lovingly reviewing my manuscript. Rakia Clark for editing my first drafts and pushing me to write more. Jessilyn Blue for the final proof. Vincent Ferguson for being my guide and accountability partner that kept me focused to the end. Victor and Ralitza Ferguson for their suggestions and comments. Jane Friedmann for typesetting.

Dr. Sandra Kennedy for giving me the Word of God concerning healing and deliverance. My Church Family for your encouragement and support during the process and most importantly to my husband, Vincent T.F. Ferguson for being by my side in and out of tribulations and difficult times.

Forward

A Killer Within, Down But Not Out is an inspiring book. Dr. Sarah Ferguson speaks of how God and His powerful Word brought her from defeat to victory through many challenges. Sarah makes a profound statement: "Difficult circumstances may be in your life, but they cannot destroy you." She is living proof of that truth. Despite life-threatening illnesses, surgeries, and even the threat of death, she refused to give up. She learned to go beyond simple knowledge of God's Word to knowing how to apply His Word in every circumstances of life and come out victorious. In her darkest hours, in the midst of mental, emotional, physical, and spiritual difficulties, she learned to turn to God for strength and encouragement. She came to know Him as Healer,

Deliverer, Redeemer, the all-knowing Supreme One. Her numerous trials and all that she learned through them can be summed up in the principle by which she has come to live: "Trust God!"

This book will inspire others to persevere in the face of hardship and put their trust in the One who is their victory.

Sarah and her family have been members of my church for many years. She played an integral part in developing guidelines and establishing our Healing Center. She and her family continue to be a vital part of our church family, and I am honored to recommend her book.

Dr. Sandra G. Kennedy
Founder and Senior Pastor
Whole Life Ministries
Augusta, GA

Table of Contents

INTRODUCTION

Fight the Good Fight of Faith

A Killer Within is about overcoming situations that are bigger than you and finding ways to thrive and improve yourself from day-to-day. This book is for anyone who has ever faced a battle in his or her life. It is about recognizing how you handle yourself in the midst of a storm. It is a look into the spiritual purification process within all of us.

"Maturing," for example, is a process. As human beings, we are forever evolving from one day to another. For each individual, what you become is a reflection of what you think and believe.

As you go through hardships, it is important to have a religious base to stand on and look up to. For me, understanding Christian biblical Scriptures has been crucial to overcoming some of the toughest times in my life. You may be in a different religion or spiritual path, but the common theme is gaining strength and purpose from God. I permitted old childhood experiences to haunt me, allowing anger and strife into my heart. I was also angry about decisions I made that the regret was killing me from within. It was difficult to move ahead with any issue.

I have seen this in other people, too; but examining the Word of God closely and figuring out how it applies to your own situation is the first step in getting past big stumbling blocks or trials.

I'm using my own life story to show you how God can work in your life. I will show you the ups and downs, and the way that God allowed me to handle them. It is my hope that the story of my experience will help you recognize when your behaviors are damaging to you. When the pain is throbbing and your head is spinning, remember the biblical Scriptures that helped me; speak them to your body and command it to fall in line. Remove the doubt by speaking the right words over yourself. Words of doubt and negativity yield nothing. The things you focus your mind on and that drive your mouth to speak are just what you will get!

God is bigger than cancer, diabetes, heart disease, and any ailment known and yet unknown to man. He is bigger than any problem you or I could ever face. As a minister of the Gospel, I had a hard time grasping and understanding this concept. However, through all of the challenges that I faced, I realized that I could trust God's Word. As a result of my pastor's continuous teaching on healing, I finally *got* it.

This book is about taking back my power to control my life. It is about changes that are necessary to survive as a wife, a mother, and a minister. Let it give you the encouragement you need to make it through your own battles. And so, let's start at the beginning – faith – because belief yields faith, and faith yields results.

Chapter 1: Faith

The First Heart Attack

It was a scorching hot day in June of 1994, and I had just finished mowing the front yard. Our family was living in Evans, Georgia while my husband Vincent was in El Salvador on a military assignment, working as a physician for the North Base Camp. It was almost 5pm and time to take Victor, my 8-year-old son, to karate practice. I made hot dogs for all of us and proceeded to the car. The karate session was only for an hour; therefore, I stayed in the car and waited while my oldest son, Vincent Jr., age 10, went to explore the hobby shop. I was feeling a little faint so I got a cold drink. I attributed the dizzy spell to the cold shower I took before leaving the house. Nothing registered as something out of the ordinary or something that required any kind of real attention.

While driving the kids back home, I remember wanting to make it home quickly so I could sit down and rest. Thank God I only lived a few miles from the karate school because traffic was horrible. Even though I was in a rush, I seemed to catch all the red lights. I could feel myself getting sicker and sicker. My head began to spin and I felt my driving skills were impaired. I made it to my driveway and struggled to get out of the car. I felt the intensity of the Georgia heat increase with each step. My mission and main objective was to get in the house and sit down! Thoughts that something was seriously wrong began to race through my head. I had never been nauseated before. *What's my problem?* I thought. *Why is my head spinning?*

Vincent Jr. ran into the house and shut off the alarm. Victor followed him, but I was still in the car. Vincent Jr. came back out to check on me. He became my human crutch to help me out of the car. We made it through the doorway and finally to a chair. Immediately upon sitting, I could no longer fight the urge to vomit and ran to the bathroom. My left arm became numb, and a deep, shooting pain entered my chest; every second the pain became deeper and stronger.

I used all my available strength to call out to Vincent Jr. He dialed 911 and ran next door to my neighbor, Marsha, who was a nurse. She recognized my symptoms as a heart attack.

I was leaning against the sink unable to move or cry out. I could hear the ambulance sirens, and I listened as Marsha gave directions. The stretcher was not going to fit in the bathroom door. I was not able to speak, but wanted to say, "Don't knock my pictures off the wall". I can't be having a heart attack! I am too young. I'm only 40, and I'm raising two children.

I thought maybe I had food poisoning or maybe it was heat exhaustion. The paramedic gave me a flavorless pill to put under my tongue. That pill seemed to blast my head open. Blood was intensely rushing through my head, but the pain in my arm and chest disappeared.

The paramedics put me on the stretcher and called the ER. "A 40-year-old woman is having a heart attack."

Those words rang in my ear.

I said to myself, "Lord, I cannot die. I am too young. I am not ready yet. Did I say my prayers today?"

The pain began to return. The crushing tightness and radiating pain into my left arm and hand was back. I was given two nitroglycerin tablets, but the pain did not subside.

The paramedics drove the ambulance in the wrong direction, wasting precious time. I remembered raising my head and telling them to go in the opposite direction to get out of the neighborhood. The tight space in the ambulance made me even sicker and I wanted to escape. I was wheeled into the emergency room quickly. I could only comprehend the bright lights and watching things whisk by me. After an examination, my diagnosis was not a heart attack, but heartburn. I was immediately discharged.

Later that night, I spoke with my husband, who was in El Salvador, and I told him what had happened and how I was feeling. He was quite concerned and frustrated that he was not physically there with me. He was suspicious of the diagnosis. I was still feeling

16

scared because the pain had returned, but all I wanted to do was sleep.

The children were already fast asleep. Betty, another neighbor, made sure that they were fed, and I reassured her that I was okay.

Brenda Barrett, my best friend from college, called and I told her all the details of the evening. She mentioned that I sounded strange. I was sounding weak and unable to maintain my concentration. I just wanted to take a shower and go to bed. Marsha was still in the house and assisted me with the shower because I could hardly raise my left arm. My arm was heavy like lead and the slightest movement caused intense pain.

The pain didn't let up but I finally fell asleep, exhausted. The next morning I heard Marsha enter the house through the back door and I heard the children at the breakfast table, but I could not move.

Marsha got me up and dressed, then drove me to the Family Practice Clinic on Fort Gordon. I heard a nurse call for help as I collapsed on a chair in the clinic.

I woke up to a middle-aged doctor standing over me and leaning into my chest with a very long needle. I only became aware of the needle when it was on its way out. It was hard to digest that a needle that size was coming out of my heart. It was filled with a blood-thinning agent that, if given to me within a certain time, would save my life.

The doctor said, "You have suffered a massive heart attack."

I felt frustrated because the symptoms were familiar. All of the symptoms were there.

I was told that I was being transported to the catheterization lab. I had no idea what that meant and was too disoriented to ask questions. My thoughts were on my children. *How can I get home?*

18

Who will raise them if something happened to me?
My husband is not in the country.

I could hear the technical chatter of the nurses and doctors. *They cannot be talking to me*, I thought. It was as if I was outside of my body listening and observing everything. While there on the table, I had an out-of-body experience. I was floating and observing. I felt I was near death and waiting on my confirmation. I saw my body lying on the table and I saw the doctors' rapid movements. I saw my lifeless body receive needles and careful treatment. While still floating, I saw the IV enter my arm and I saw the doctors frantically do chest compressions. I heard a clear voice that said, "Go back..." I abruptly awoke to the doctor standing over me with the unfamiliar needle in my chest. *What is going on?*

As I regained consciousness, I began to be bombarded with acronyms and unfamiliar medical terminology.

What is CCICU? Who are they talking about? If only my husband was here. He could help me understand the medical code. I was still in shock and in disbelief that I had had a heart attack. "Heart attack" was the only decipherable communication that kept ringing in my head.

Marsha contacted the Red Cross and they sent an emergency message to my husband in El Salvador. The message read: "Proceed to Augusta, Georgia on the next flight to the United States. Your wife is in grave condition." My husband was very concerned because he just had a conversation with me the night before and was still suspicious of the initial diagnosis.

The next few days were a blur. I wanted to get up out of bed and go home. I was *still* in denial of what had just occurred. A nurse came into my room and started fussing at me because I was in the mirror curling my hair.

She kept saying, "Mrs. Ferguson you have had a massive heart attack!"

I wanted to leave the hospital no matter what anyone was saying. I became angry on the inside because of my failing health. This could not be *me*; I am too young and too healthy. Yet, I harbored feelings of stress and anxiety. The kids said I would "fuss" for any reason. Any little thing would have sent me spinning. Typically, I would come home and lash out on the kids. It could be that there were two dishes left unwashed in the sink, too many lights left on, or the dog knocked over something and they had to clean it up. Whatever it was, I would go from zero to 50 in seconds, screaming. My children eventually became numb to the whole cycle.

I could not grasp the seriousness of it all. After three days, I was adamant about going home; I signed myself out of the clinic against medical orders. I didn't want to hear or listen to what my husband Vince, or the doctors had to say. I was going to do what I wanted to do. I was in complete denial. Proverbs 1:7 says, "The fear of the Lord is the beginning of knowledge; but fools despise wisdom and instructions." I despised what the doctors were saying, they were telling me the truth. I wanted my life to go on as usual.

I wanted to say the Lord's Prayer, but my mind would not cooperate. I was so confused. I forgot how to pray; yet I knew that God had saved me from death. I remember whispering, "Jesus, I survived!"

I went right back to work a week after my brush with death. It was business as usual. I did not want to rest. I felt re-energized to complete my assigned projects before I died. Vince could not convince me to stay home and rest. I spent most of that time refusing to accept that anything had ever happened or that there was any difference in my health. My husband tried his best to convince me otherwise, but again I simply did not want to hear it. My stubbornness was reinforced because I felt stronger each day.

My son Vincent Jr. was fearful that he would not be prepared if another heart attack or emergency occurred. He feared that something could happen if he did the wrong thing. He felt he had to be prepared to drive me to the hospital, if necessary. He had to know all the symptoms of something being wrong with me. In addition, he had to take care of his younger brother. Sports became his outlet; it was an escape from the expectations of school and the responsibility of being home. He was always a good athlete and sports helped him stay focused and balanced. As a result of the first heart attack, Vincent thought that I would display a change in my lifestyle, but I had quickly forgotten that it had happened and returned back to my same old routines.

Today, I know that I had all the warning signs (risk factors) for having a heart attack. I carried a lot of stress and a lot of anger: anger about my childhood, anger over mishaps in my life, and anger over personal choices. I even had issues with wanting to please others. The Bible is very clear about holding onto anger. In Ephesians 4:26-27, it instructs us to "Be ye angry, and sin not; let not the sun go down upon your wrath (anger, rage, resentment, fury, displeasures and annoyance). Neither give place to the devil."

I was making some poor decisions that would later greatly affect my life and quality of life. I thought I could manipulate situations and control people. I neglected myself, and was robbing myself of the possibility of long life; in turn, I was robbing my family of more time with me. I had to be in control. The Bible calls this witchcraft (Galatians 5:19-20). I needed deliverance! My situation began to turn around after spending hours and days before the Lord. I had to have a one-on-one encounter with God. I used meditation on the Word of God, chewing and digesting the Word. It was necessary for me to ponder and chew the Word of God over and over. Yes. I was ready to preach and teach others... but not so willing to change myself. You could say I was un-teachable at that time. I was convinced that the ministry needed me.

My co-workers and I took an old grocery store and converted it into a community center focused on aiding children and the homeless. A local Methodist Church provided most of the labor and materials. At one point, I had all of the children in the neighborhood doing community service. We had walls to paint, old groceries to clear away, and a drug-infested parking lot to clear. The revamped facility housed the ministry, which provided counseling, job interviewing skills, clothes, and school supplies for children. It also doubled as a center for the needy.

I had responsibilities for the maintenance of the facility in addition to the fundraising. This project consumed most of my time from 1991 to 1993. I would work in the center, come home and cook, take the children to their lessons, and then put them to bed. After they were down for the night, I would work on paperwork until nearly 2 a.m. While my husband was working, this was my regular routine. I got very little rest. I was consumed and overwhelmed with this project. I was selfishly invested in the success of this ministry. I placed the needs of my ministry above my personal upkeep. I neglected my physical health.

Stress was a normal part of my day, although the Bible says in Philippians 4:6, "Do not fret or have any anxiety about anything, but in every circumstance and in everything, by prayer and petition, (definite requests) with thanksgiving, continue to make your wants known to God." (AMP)

I spent only a few moments a day in prayer and studying God's Word. I was more invested in *doing* things, rather than applying God's Words to my life. I was motivated by the approval of man, and I did everything possible to get the attention I craved.

The Bible says in 2 Timothy 2:15 to study to show yourself approved, rightly dividing the Word of truth. My studying was limited at that time. My focus was on raising the kids, taking care of the household, and taking care of the ministry. My life was about going to church, listening to a message and going home. My relationship with God was lacking what I needed to survive a storm.

Defining Faith

Faith is believing in something that you cannot see. Hebrews 11:1 tells us, "Now faith is the substance of things hoped for, the evidence of things not seen." Additionally, Webster's Dictionary defines faith as "belief in, devotion to, or trust in somebody or something, especially without logical proof." The Bible says in Hebrews 11:6 that, "without Faith it is impossible to please God." We were created to have a relationship with God, which is strengthened by faith. Faith is the reality of 1 Peter 5:7, which advises us to cast our cares on the Lord. It believes it long before you see it.

I first learned these things as a child in my hometown of Dade City, Florida. The rule at my Baptist church was that you had to be at least eight or nine to be considered "of age;" meaning, you were able to accept Christ as your Lord and Savior and you understood your decision. I learned about Jesus in Sunday school and got saved at age nine during a revival. I became a youth leader and began delivering messages to the congregation at age 16. I *believed* and I accepted what the preacher taught.

And what is that exactly?

Well, the Holy Trinity is God the Father, Jesus Christ the Son and the Holy Spirit. Once we receive Jesus Christ as our personal Savior, our Spirits are born again. It is our soul that has to be renewed.

The body is the "house" in which we live. It will grow older daily. God has given us instructions on what to do with our bodies. It is the body that suffers with disease and sickness. It is the body that is sick, not the Spirit. Without a relationship with God, a person faced with catastrophic illness can quickly lose their will to live because they do not have a relationship with their Spirit.

When facing personal obstacles, I have turned to God for strength and encouragement. On my darkest days, I knew of no other person to turn to. He's forgiven me of my sins and put me on the road to recovery, both physically and emotionally. With Him in my life, I readily adopt a heart of gratitude. I appreciate life. He is the Great I Am, the Strong One, the Father of Creation, the Holy One, the Merciful One, and the All-Knowing and Supreme Being, Jehovah is His name. You must have relationship with God. I have come to know Him as my Healer, Deliverer, and Redeemer. I had to make up in my mind and spirit that He is God, and above Him there is no other. He is the Master of the Word, the Lord my provider, the Lord my Shepherd, the Lord of Peace, and much more. He has revealed Himself in my life. I simply *believe* that there is a God, a Supreme Being.

That is what I learned as a girl, and that is what I believe today. It has been the deciding factor to all the major decisions I've ever made, including my marriage to Vincent Ferguson in 1980. After a year of marriage, we both decided that we were ready for children. Although it was our plan, it was not yet God's plan. We experienced a miscarriage early in our marriage that made us wonder if I was capable of carrying a baby full term. My husband and I were both people of faith but doubt still remained present. In 1982, by the grace of God we had a seven-pound baby boy! Two years later we were once again faced with the pain of another miscarriage. The familiar pain and frustration returned. Despite our human feelings, we continued to believe in God's plan. We tried again and we were blessed with an eight-pound baby boy.

Through my difficulties as a youth, I found God to be faithful. My spiritual foundation was established early in my life and continued into my marriage. I survived a multitude of family tragedies and personal struggles. I am a *SURVIVOR!*

As Christians, we believe in the existence of God. However, our faith can fail us sometimes. Because faith is a gift from God, He continues to strengthen it by allowing troubles in our lives that sharpen our belief. This is confirmed in the Scriptures.

James 1:3 (NIV) says, "...because you know that the testing of your faith produces perseverance." We must know that God is working behind the scenes on our behalf, even when there is no tangible evidence to support the fact. That is how faith works.

Faith vs. Fear

Faith is the opposite of fear. It must be understood that fear is a spiritual force. Having fear keeps you in bondage. Fear is a tool used by the enemy, Satan. The name Satan can be difficult for some people to hear and even to accept, but he is a spiritual being that must be recognized. People who aren't religious can often accept that there may be a God, but Satan is often left out of the conversation entirely. Satan gains power by not being recognized as a negative influence in the lives of man. Fear gives Satan access to your life. When you are not aware of Satan's tactics and schemes, you can forget that there is a promise of God that covers your life. Keep in mind that the enemy's primary goal is to get you to doubt that God's Word is true or to keep you ignorant of God's Word.

Primarily we live in a fear-filled world, where being fearful is normal. Accordingly, 2 Timothy 1:7 says that God did not give us the spirit of fear, but that He gives us power, love and a sound mind. (KJV) You may ask what causes us to fear? Fear keeps you in a "spirit of bondage." We all have experienced fear in one way or another. There is fear of people's opinions, fear of being alone, and fear of speaking. There are all types of things that have their root from fear; all fear leads to bondage. In fact, fear keeps you in a spirit of bondage. These are the things that keep us depressed and anxious. Webster's Dictionary defines bondage as "the condition of being involuntarily subject to a power, force, or influence."

God wants us to not be a people of fear, but to have faith. The Scripture plainly says, "Have faith in God."

Even a small amount of faith can accomplish big things. God requires for us to have a small degree of faith; the size of a mustard seed. Just a little faith will do. Matthew 17:20 says, "And Jesus said unto them, Because of your unbelief: for verily I say unto you, If ye have faith as a grain of mustard seed, ye shall say unto this mountain, Remove hence to yonder place; and it shall remove; and nothing shall be impossible unto you."

I had to believe that God was God and he had already conquered disease. I was going after my healing. Just a "little" faith will work. A little faith can accomplish *big* things. I realized that things could have easily gone wrong, yet God gave me another chance. Many days I would sing songs and hymns unto the Lord. I increased my prayer and praise time. During praise time I was showing thanks, however, when I moved into worship I was honoring God for being God.

Fear is the big giant that keeps us from believing what God has already said. Fear "is False Evidence Appearing Real." Fear will keep you from accomplishing your goal. It could be buying a house, getting a new job, getting delivered from drug abuse, or receiving your healing; all of these are simple tasks for the Almighty God. All we have to do is to *believe*. Mark 11:24 says, "Therefore I say unto you, what things so ever ye desire, when ye pray, believe that ye receive *them*, and ye shall have *them*."

It is a journey. All experiences will lead to an expected end... I win.

Dealing with Overachievement

It was the year 1972 and the final days for High School seniors in Dade City, Florida. An awards ceremony was planned to celebrate the students' achievements during the school year. I was so excited about it that I told every one of my family members to be there. My homeroom teacher informed me that I would be getting an award. This was most important to me because I had spent the year representing the State of Florida as Vice President of Projects for the Future Homemakers of America (FHA). It was a milestone for a young, black woman from the Deep South. At the time, my high school was newly integrated. In fact, my class was the first to graduate after the mandatory change in government law that gave black students the right to attend white schools.

Previously, black students attended their neighborhood schools and had achievements and all kinds of sports accolades, but academically, we struggled. Many times, high achieving minorities students didn't attain academic accolades because of test results that were sometimes altered. No one would talk about it publically. I attended a segregated high school during my freshman and sophomore years. We would have a big Christmas parade for the city, and the white schools would go first in the parade. The black schools were forced to the back of the parade and placed directly behind the horses. We had to march through the constant barrage of horse manure because no one cared to pick it up before the black bands marched past. This is just one example of the flagrant racism that existed at that time. School board members were afraid that any incident would spark a riot. The times were tumultuous.

When the Civil Rights laws changed, both Blacks and Whites had skepticism about the situation, resulting in some people not willing to make the change. In my hometown Dade City, Florida, Blacks still had to enter the theater through the back staircase. We still had to walk around the back of a restaurant to receive service.

When the downtown lunch counter was integrated, most Blacks were still afraid to sit down for service. The pharmacy had a lunch counter where you could buy ice cream, hamburgers, and other quick food items. Blacks could order, but had to receive their food at the end of the counter and could not sit to eat or wait. Whites were always served first. It didn't matter if there was a line or not. If you wanted food, you knew the rules.

The awards ceremony began at 10:00 a.m., and I was on pins and needles. The first awards went to the valedictorian and salutatorian. Then each department chairperson had to present awards. "Sarah Jefferson!" the announcer called. I went to the stage in total astonishment. The award was for Voice of Democracy, a contest for a written and oratorical presentation. Finally, it was time for the Future Homemaker of America's award to be announced. I was recognized again for being elected to the highest rank of officers on the state level. This brought

statewide attention to my school. At the end of the awards ceremony, I ended up receiving thirteen awards and scholarships!

During the awards ceremony, the principal asked for the parents to stand and be recognized. Unfortunately, no one was there to represent me. The shock of finding out that no one was there was too much. I immediately ran from the stage and hid in the girl's bathroom. I was grateful that one of the teachers stood up and received the applause from the audience on my behalf. It turned out that my aunt, who I loved and respected, had simply forgotten about the award program. My mother did not come to the awards ceremony because she did not care. I heard that she told her friends that she had no intention of "going up there with those white folks." She and I never talked about it, but the people in the neighborhood were critical of her missing my big moment. The Black teachers were outraged about the lack of interest from my family. Even the drunks on the street gave me money to finance my college career. I received praise from everyone in the community. They were proud of me.

To help me get to college, I received gift certificates and cash from friends, family members, and local businesses and churches. I didn't take the money home with me because I knew that my mother would have found ways to spend it. I kept the gifts and gratuities in a secret room at my aunt's house. Shortly after the awards ceremony, I went to live with my aunt; for many years, I did not spend a night at my mother's house. I was bitter and angry that she did not support my academic talent. So I stayed with my aunt and bit by bit, I gathered what I needed to start college. By the end of the summer, I was ready. I even had a Lady Baltimore luggage set which was special to me because I did not know any Black people who owned such expensive luggage. The community purchased the best for me.

I went to Johnson C. Smith University in Charlotte, NC, and I ended up getting a full academic scholarship. As I matriculated through college, I became an introvert. I was hurt and disappointed in people. I had deep trust issues. I didn't want to get hurt by anyone else. I only participated in the university choir. This is where I met my best friend and sister, Brenda Dunmeyer Barrett. She was my roommate and I felt that I could trust her. Nobody had ever been that kind to me. Her mother adopted me as her daughter. Brenda's mother requested that we always stay together and that is when Brenda and I made a pact to always be there for each other.

I received my BA degree in three years in Business Administration. Each semester in college I took 18-20 credits and worked. I worked for a local department store in Dade City as an assistant to the bookkeeper. I worked during the spring break and Christmas holidays. I didn't know it at the time, but the store owner only paid me half of my wage for years. After he caught wind of the terrible things that my mother had done to me, he gave me the remaining balance of the wages I should have been paid from the start. People I least expected began to look out for me. I also earned money from working at fast food restaurant. I was happy to have saved most of my money in a bank account.

I bought my first car during the second year of my college journey. I went home with enough money to purchase a new car off of the showroom floor. It was an amazing feeling to know that I had done this on my own. I didn't have to wait on permission. I knew no one could take the car away from me. I had earned it. By the Grace of God, it was mine! My aunt told me not to pay the full amount for the car except for $1,000 to establish credit. My monthly payment was $62. What great advice! This was the beginning of me wanting to please myself and take care of myself. It was at this point that I found the determination to be the best in every area of my life. I wanted to continue to gain approval again from others. I wanted to hear, "Well done, Sarah." To achieve a "B" in a subject was just not good enough for me. I became infatuated with the rush that accomplishing my goals gave me. I no longer wanted to be the victim, knowing that I had the strength within me to overcome any obstacle.

Through meditation on the Word of God, I learned the meaning of Matthew 6:23: "But seek ye first the kingdom of God, and His righteousness; and all these things shall be added unto you." This Scripture set the priorities for my life, and it is one of the Scriptures that my aunt, Mary Marshall, drilled into me. She would emphasize the importance of learning more about God, and establishing a relationship that would change my life. The more I studied God's Word, the more I understood the meaning of "seek Him first."

During my junior and senior years of college, I completed an internship with an insurance company in the actuary department. It was the most boring job I had ever done, but luckily I discovered the claims department. In claims, there was excitement, interaction and conversation among the employees. This was when I first realized that I needed a job that involved people; not a job sitting in a quiet environment that would drive me crazy. This realization played an important role in my career choices later on.

After graduation, I was hired full time in 1976 as a claims adjuster. I had to deal with people who faced adverse situations. They were agitated before I even began to speak to them. People were usually upset over their vehicle, and they wanted an immediate response. However, I had to first establish liability on the part of the insured. This required a great deal of diplomacy and empathy. The problem was that I did not have one claim to deal with. I had up to 12 a day that required my attention. Some of the accidents involved injuries and property damage.

My specialty was Tort Liability, injuries, slip and falls and serious accidents. The job was extremely stressful and required quick assessments and resolutions. I had to maintain my cool even when I wanted to blow my top. The average duration for that job is three years. However, I managed to perform my duties for that job for five years.

Each day was like no other; I would always have more claims than I could handle. New claims would be assigned to me, and there were always follow-up assignments.

I had no idea the level of stress that I was putting my body through. Years later, I came to realize the consequences for my behavior.

When a client approached and was difficult to deal with, I had to put them at ease and inform them constantly that everything would work out. Some people would even try to curse me out. No matter what they said, I had to present self-control. I grew angry sometimes on the inside. Anger produces harmful emotions and most sickness can be a result of anger. It is a root and produces harmful emotions.

I discovered that dealing with anger starts as a spiritual problem and then as a natural problem. Anger is when you cannot get the other person to do what you want or to convince them that they are wrong. I now realize that I have to be concerned about what goes into my heart because the heart is like a garden. Whatever goes into your heart will multiply. If you're not careful, suppressed anger will show its ugly head without warning. It can be a killer from within.

With my insurance job, I was angry at the amount of paperwork that I had to do and the brief amount of time that I had to do it. Frustration entered when management and others took notice of all the things I did not do and didn't recognize things I did do. At work, I had to pretend like my anger and frustration were not real. It felt like being in a small square box that I couldn't push my way out of. I had to maintain my reputation of perfection at all costs! I believed perfect people are not supposed to get mad or show negative feelings. Yet, sometimes I would explode on someone for no reason. Ephesians 4:26 tell us to "not let the sun go down on your anger." I needed to be emotionally free. My life was being ruled by anger, and I had to repent. Proverbs 16:31 tell us "to be quick to hear and slow to speak." I had to express myself. I wanted to express myself, but didn't. I would pretend as if I was not angry on the inside but I would constantly talk about the negative things that happened at work to my friends. I was deceiving myself.

A perceived lack of power was the source of my anger. It was driven by fear. It was fear of the unknown and fear of rejections. Negative emotions caused me to make bad decisions. I lacked self-control. Anger was like a poison spreading rapidly through my body. I had allowed fear and bitterness to set in. I certainly did not know how to cope and I was too proud to ask for help.

One day in 1981, my husband came home and said he was on active duty after medical school. I had forgotten he was even in the army, but that is who paid for his medical school. The next few days we were assigned a new duty station in Fayetteville, NC. I had no idea what to expect. I knew absolutely nothing about the army. We were later assigned to a base in Germany. I did not work the first year, but later resumed a career as an employment coordinator. In that position, I would offer employment information to the spouses of active-duty personnel. I went off the grid of normal business hours and established a teen program for the community. The teens would provide services as babysitters, pet walkers, car washers, and cleaners. I would work six days a week, giving up my Saturdays to supervise the car washes. The youths learned how to set up bank accounts and make payroll. My sons had a good time working right alongside the teens.

I enjoyed this program. It got me out of the office and I was able to formulate and implement ideas immediately. It was refreshing and rewarding. I was given the opportunity to present this program to the Department of the Army nationwide. The program was called Hire-a-Teen. It became a functional program throughout the military bases worldwide. I performed this job for more than two years when an employment opportunity came my way to manage a program offering employment counseling to soldiers, who were exiting the military due to downsizing of troops. I took on the responsibility of handling the contract side of the program called ACAP, Army Career Alumni Program.

As Job Assistance Site Manager, I was responsible for establishing the program from the beginning stages. I was loaded with the responsibility of doing this in a foreign country. I purchased supplies, furniture, set up computers, managed a large budget and hired the staff to maintain the program. As part of my responsibilities, I had to travel; this kept me away from home frequently.

When I was at home, I was tired and irritable, taking it all out on my family. It was a joy to provide the much-needed services, yet stressful to my body. One summer day, I was taken to the nearby hospital with numbness on the left side and chest pains. This was the beginning of my heart problems. Unfortunately, they did not do an echocardiogram and only said I had a panic attack. They did detect a heart murmur and indicated that I should keep an eye on it. I had no idea what this meant, just that the pain had ceased and I wanted to be discharged. I immediately immersed myself back into the same stressful environment that landed me in the hospital in the first place. I lived for the adrenaline rush of accomplishment. I loved to create and be the trailblazer.

The job had taken a physical toll on my body, but I was so thankful for the opportunity to provide employment information to the soldiers and their family. I had great pride in knowing that my staff sent a soldier back home prepared to go into the regular job force.

I thought I was happy and pleased with my accomplishments. I wanted to do my *best*.

Chapter 2: The Drive to Keep Fighting

The Second Heart Attack

In September of 1994, my family and I went to Tybee Island for a weekend outing. We enjoyed Tybee Island, which is outside of Savannah, Georgia. My beach activities were listening to and watching the tide come in and then return back to the big, wide ocean.

The incoming tide represents the problems and struggles in my life. Then there is the promise from God that I am never alone. God is always with me. The outgoing tide washes out the old for the new. It amazes me how God created the ocean. Most things inside of it depend on the flow of the tide. To this day, I consider this to be my alone time with God. I seem to get so much inspiration while relaxing on the beach.

I walked alone on the beach for hours while my husband Vince took care of the children. Upon returning from my walk, we went to the Shrimp Factory, my favorite restaurant on the river. They served the best food and the most amazing coffee.

After eating, we decided to walk and to explore the shops along the river. Once we returned to the hotel room, we got ready for bed. The children fell out from exhaustion, and in no time flat, they were sleeping.

I laid down on the bed with my husband, but I was unable to fall asleep. Pain started in my arm and rotated to my chest. It was a constant dull pain. I was unable to catch my breath. This time I recognized what was happening to me—another heart attack.

I woke my husband up and he called 911. The ambulance came without oxygen and nitroglycerin because they were fire and rescue only. I began to yell at them because they were not prepared to handle my emergency. Each panicky word I yelled caused the pain to increase. I could not believe that they were not prepared! This was an ambulance! Somehow I had to calm myself down. They realized it was going to take us 20 minutes to drive across the bridge to the nearest hospital. All I could think to do was to pray.   I couldn't believe that this was happening again! I was wondering who was going to watch the children while my husband and I went to the hospital, but God always sends an angel to help us in times of trouble. There was a desk supervisor at the hotel that agreed to keep an eye on them. We woke up our oldest son and told him what was happening. The instructions were to take care of his younger brother, who was sleeping through the whole ordeal.

Where is the nearest hospital? Are we there yet? These were the questions screaming inside me. I heard the radio communication to the hospital. The hospital doctor quickly gave orders to the EMTs. They were prepared for my arrival. I do not remember much about the treatment or what happened after we arrived at the hospital. I passed out.

I was startled when I woke up. The doctor confirmed I had another heart attack. He wanted to do open-heart surgery immediately. I didn't want them to do it in Savannah because we were far away from home and it was important for me to be around family and friends. I knew from the first heart attack that I needed assistance in rehabilitating. I couldn't have surgery here.

The on-call doctor in Savannah began to work with the Dr. Farley Neasman, the cardiologist at Eisenhower, to arrange for my transportation home. I kept adamantly insisting that they transport me as soon as possible. They had to make sure that I was stable enough to travel. They arranged for a transport vehicle with a nurse on board for me. Everyone was concerned that I would die during the two-hour ride to Eisenhower. I had to take the risk. The nurse was armed with a defibrillator, oxygen, and a blood thinner. By the grace of God, we finally made it and I was immediately taken to the catheterization lab again. This time I knew what the CATH Lab was all about so it was less scary. It is an operating room with large television screens for the doctors to review the blockages in the heart. It looked like something from a spacecraft. Very intimidating. The lights were extremely bright and the room smelled of antiseptic.

The doctor inserted a small rod filled with dye inside my body to get a clearer picture of what was happening within me. He was the same doctor who put the needle in my chest during the first heart attack. This time I was fully alert and could see on screen the damage that was done by it. The damage was in the left ventricle.   Now I was able to see the new blockage on the right side of my heart.

The doctors were astonished that I was still alive. No one seemed to understand how my heart was still pumping; the blockage was so severe, *doctors didn't understand it.* It was a miracle! He put in a stint, which is a small bridge that holds the blood vessels together. I watched myself go through this operation. I couldn't see the needles as they completed the stint. I also saw the dye pump through my heart on-screen. The dye allowed the doctors to see the blood flow of my heart. I stayed in the hospital for four days. This time I waited on the doctors to release me. No more breaking out of the hospital.

I managed to stay out of the hospital for a few weeks following the surgery. During that time I went to cardiac rehabilitation weekly. This procedure involved an exercise routine and walking. After about three weeks, I was back in the hospital with angina. I was again experiencing pain in my chest and left arm. I was evaluated to rule out the possibility of a third heart attack. Lying in the hospital bed, I felt like an elephant was on my chest that was holding my breathing down. I discovered later on if you have chest pains and difficulty breathing, then you are admitted to the hospital for a minimum of three days. Patients are given blood tests and monitoring. This is a regular hospital policy for anyone with chest pain.

Upon leaving the hospital, I went back to doing my usual activities. I wanted to stay involved in everything. I wanted to be near the action. I worked in the church and took care of my husband and children. I did not rest or take it easy as instructed. Again, I was not listening to anything anybody was saying. I wanted to keep doing things my way.

Dr. Neasman even gave me a stress personality test revealing that I was an overachiever. I was off the scale on my stress level. I was fragile, but kept up a strong front that I had everything under control.

I blamed everyone except myself for my situation. From my childhood to adulthood, I wanted everyone else to be at fault for the things that had happened in my life. I did not want to take responsibility for myself and the decisions I made. I didn't want to pay attention to myself.

I went in and out of depression. My emotions went from one extreme to another. There were days that I would confess God's Word and feel encouraged by the Word. Then other days I would be a basket case. I wrote a letter to Lavone Hicks, my friend from college. In this letter, I told her what I wanted her to do once I died. I requested that she sing a special song. She came to Augusta to encourage me not give up. She said, "I refuse to let you die on me. No! I will not sing a song over you."

After a spiritual encounter with God and my friend, I no longer wanted to give up. I had made up in my mind that I wanted to see my grandchildren and my great-grandchildren. I got better over time. The thought of giving up was not an option. I had made up in my mind that I was going to fight.

It was at this time that my husband and I changed churches and united under a ministry that taught about healing. It was at Whole Life Ministries in Augusta, Georgia where I learned how to apply the Word of God to my situation and to my life. Prior to that time, I was only being preached to, and not letting the Word of God embellish my spirit. I wasn't taking personal actions toward my healing.

Hear the word: The Word of God is the Will of God. We often want to ask the question, "What is the will of God?" or "Is this God's will for me to be sick?" The answer is in the Scriptures.

An example of Jesus going about teaching, *healing*, and delivering is found in the story when Jesus healed the lame man by the pool (John 5: 5-16).

There was a lame man lying at the pool of Bethesda waiting to be healed. A great number of disabled people were also there. The blind, the lame, and the paralyzed jumped into the pool while the waters were being stirred. It was their belief that the healing power in the water stirred it.

When Jesus saw the lame man lying by the pool and He learned that he had been in this condition for 38 years, He asked him, "Do you want to get well?"

The man began to offer excuses as to why he could not get healed. "I have no one to help," he replied. How many times do we make excuses for not being healed? What could the lame man have done differently? We all want healing, but we don't want to believe.

Jesus said to him, "Get up! Pick up your mat and walk."

Instantly, the man was cured. He picked up his mat and walked away. The man had the opportunity to become spiritually healed, as well as physically healed. Jesus is still in the healing business.

Believe It before You See It

Many times I wanted to do *nothing*. It was too hard to put my faith to work. How does one make his/her faith work? It is not easy. The first step is simple. Settle on the fact that there is someone greater than you who exists in the universe. God sets things in motion for us to live out a complete and full life. The Bible says that Jesus came to give us life and for us to have it more abundantly. John 10:10 further states that there is a thief (known as the Devil) that comes to steal, and to kill, and to destroy. That is why we have to stand and fight back. It is like a prizefighter getting ready for a match. He has to see himself in the middle of the fight, winning with each blow. He must anticipate each punch and react!

You cannot back down on the Word of God. You should always keep it steadfast in your mind, and make confessions with your lips. You cannot afford to stand still and do nothing because the enemy will destroy you. The hardest part in this process is to believe it before it is manifested. Some may wonder and question how can you work through what you feel or think? How can you do this?

The only way to do it is to persuade your mind into going beyond what is happening and what you are feeling. If you are not careful, your emotions will have you going in many directions. Yes, it seemed to me as if things were going in the wrong directions, but God had other plans for my life. I had to first get control of my emotions.

Understanding the Struggle

James 1:3 says, "Be assured *and* understand that the trial *and* proving of your faith bring out endurance *and* steadfastness *and* patience." You cannot afford to give up. Circumstances may be in your life but they cannot destroy you. Some may wonder and question how can you combat the pain you feel? *The only way to do it is to train your mind into going beyond what is happening and what you are feeling.*

My physical condition was so far misaligned with my belief that I was healed. I would cry because I felt like my faith was not working. The pain kept radiating throughout my body and canceling out my belief that I was healed. I kept asking myself how can I increase my faith? I thought that constant prayer would lead to my healing, but God simply wanted me to trust in Him. Yes, it seemed to me as if things were going in the wrong direction, but God had other plans for my life. Personally, step one was gaining control of my emotions. There were so many things that ended up being for my own good. I developed more patience; I realized that I had great endurance and will to stay alive. I learned how to be kind, and to put others' needs ahead of my own.

I used the Scripture in Isaiah 41:10: "Fear not (there is nothing to fear), for I am with you; do not look around you in terror and be dismayed, for I am your God. I will strengthen and harden you to difficulties, yes, I will help you; yes, I will hold you up and retain you with my (victorious) right hand of rightness and justice." (AMP)

Many doctors have observed miraculous healing from patients who had faith that their struggle was temporary and healing was possible. People who are not spiritual believers often require a quantitative analysis of how healing might work. Statistics and faith don't play well with each other. Past outcomes and predictability go out the window when God is involved. It is easy to identify inconsistencies in situations that faith-based people consider miracles.

God has also given man free will. He will not override your personal will to live or die. Step two was *believing*.

Chapter 3: Jesus Did it All for Us

<u>Faith in Action</u>

To wonder or feel puzzled indicates that you are not trusting God. How big is your God? Do you trust Him to work things out? We cannot receive by faith if we keep on wondering "what if." It will inhibit us from receiving God. It will also hinder our prayers unto God. Believe that you will receive it.

My first manifestation of a healing was not physical. Instead, God chose to heal the relationship between my mother and I. God taught me how to respect her. Because of God's Word to honor thy mother and father, I never disrespected her position. My aunt taught me to honor her.

Growing up with my mother was hazardous. She did not know how to discipline. As a result, she administered beatings for minor incidents. There were routine beatings with an extension cord, belts, tree limbs or what ever else was available. Punishment would be for not cleaning up the kitchen or for not turning off the lights. Many of my peers knew about the beatings and the abuse, but they could not do anything about the situation. Beatings were an accepted form of punishment when I was growing up. The police would not get involved, and I did not remember ever hearing anything about social services. The worst part was being awakened from a sound sleep by someone standing over me, beating me.

There are still times when I wake up screaming from nightmares. My childhood memories often replay themselves in my dreams.

I understand now that my mother did not know how to teach me obedience. She had many unresolved personal issues. There was no government or social agency help for a mother during that time period.

After my heart attacks, God allowed my mother and Ito converse on a new level. We sat alone in a room and I began to confess my childhood memories to her. I was able to be honest with the recollection of my childhood. I had not shared my experience with others and had kept my emotions internal. Anger and resentment towards my mother had become a part of who I was, even if it was not outwardly expressed. After hours of uninterrupted conversation, she apologized for being an abusive parent and showed me love. I left the room feeling fulfilled and complete. I left her to be alone, as she continued to pray.

Upon my return to the room, she requested to reaffirm her walk with Christ. She was a churchgoer, but not a doer of the Word. In her later months, she developed an intimate relationship with Christ. She came for a visit. In the four weeks that she stayed with my family in Augusta, she learned and yearned for more of my pastor's teachings. Until the day that she died, she continued to study the word.

As a child I learned the Scripture "seek ye first the kingdom of God and then all others things will be added onto you." (Matthew 6:33).

How do you instruct someone to believe? Well, think of it this way: when you go to sit in a chair, you just know that the chair will hold you. You have faith that it is constructed to hold your weight. Hoping in Christ is the same. We know that we know. We know He is a healer. I know that the price for my healing has already been paid.

Why Lord? Why Me?

You cannot figure out the "why." We call it reasoning, when people spend time trying to figure out the "why." We are not capable as humans to understand God. We can easily disobey a directive from the Lord because a situation does not make sense or seem logical. We may also be tempted to not believe God and dismiss His instruction. We hear from God through the Scriptures, dreams and visions. He will also speak to us in a quiet voice when we are still.

With each heart attack, I had to take a stand. I could have had a pity party. It would have been easy to give up. I had to decide if I believed in the Scriptures and in what God says, or if I would only believe the doctors' reports. I could not doubt that I would be healed. I knew that it was going to be a fight. I had to make a declaration that I wanted to live. It was a fight that would have ended in death, if I had not fought. I had to get up off the mat and go at it again. I had to speak that I was healed and speak it loud. I had to convince my body of what my spirit had already said. I was healed. This was not easy. There were times that I floated between belief and doubt. I just kept on saying out loud what the Scripture said. *I am healed!*

Proverbs 18:21 (NIV) says, "The tongue has the power of life and death." This means that the tongue has creative power. Sooner or later it will produce that which was spoken. We speak positive and negative things over ourselves daily. We may utter such a comment as, "My head hurts." With this type of expression, you have just spoken a condemning situation over yourself. Even when we think we are just being playful, our words are heard by our bodies.

Expressions like, "I was scared to death," can create a physical consequence that is associated with "death." It can be a blessing or a curse, depending on the words spoken.

At no point should you give up and throw in the towel. I knew that I could not give up. For one thing, I had two young children to raise. Secondly, I wanted more time with my husband. I had more ministry to do. I was too young to give up and throw in the towel. It was my choice if I lived or died. You may have to back up and re-examine the situation from a different angle, but never give up. Galatians 6:9: "And let us not be weary in well doing; for in due season we shall reap, if we faint not." I knew that if I had given up, the Lord would grant my wish and take me on home to be with Jesus. I don't believe He would've overridden my will. The enemy wants me to choose death. Life *and* death is in the power of *my* tongue. The enemy wants me to choose death.

I had to continue the fight with God's grace and Word. When you want to give up, just remember that you have Almighty God as your coach. He is cheering for you to stay in the fight. He is there to strengthen you and give you the fortitude not to give up. My anxiety and frustration almost caused me to have a nervous breakdown. My family didn't even know what my mental state was. I really didn't know the level of my stress until doctors ran a test that showed I was deep into depression.

I read a lot of books on healing and deliverance that helped, but I needed to have my mind clear and free from junk. I had been carrying around other people's junk and baggage for years! I had to get back up and continue to fight! *I was fighting for my life!* Ephesians 6:16 says, "Above all, taking the shield of faith, wherewith ye shall be able to quench all the fiery darts of the wicked." The process may seem slow, but things are turning with each blow to the enemy. Remember that this battle is not ours, but the Lord's, and he has already won. So see yourself as a winner, too.

1 Timothy 6:12 says, "Fight the good fight of faith... Stay in the match, fight with your faith." You have to keep fighting.

The Price Paid on Calvary

Have you ever wondered if God loves you? Do your circumstances ever cause you to question God's love for you? I did. I had to press in and research God's love for me. I began by reading the book of John and discovered just how much He loved me. I found out that he is involved in every aspect of my life. The Bible says that he is aware of every hair on my head. That includes the gray ones and the dyed ones. Even in the midst of the most difficult circumstances, God's love is real in our life. Nothing can ever separate you from His love; nothing can ever cause Him to love you less (see Romans 8:35-39). I often wondered how a mighty God could love me. I did not think I was deserving of such love. I kept reading and reading the Scriptures, and I found out that I didn't do anything to deserve such love. It is a gift from God. It is called grace and mercy. The 23rd Psalm says "grace and mercy shall follow me all the days of my life." I just decided to believe that.

I believed and received God's love. He sacrificed His only son to pay the price for my sins and to give me the freedom to experience His goodness.

It was important for me to get an understanding of what my healing was all about. It is amazing to me when someone says that they do not believe in God. Faced with death, I knew my only choice was to turn to God. It is a choice whether you believe in God or not. How can you not believe there is a God when you just look around and see His awesome power?

Between my pain and suffering, I was learning. I had to get things together in my mind. I knew that if my mind was "renewed," I would stand a better chance of surviving the storm I faced. Remember, there was nothing wrong with my spirit. The mind tells the body what to do. To look the devil in the eye, we must know what privileges we have as a result of Calvary, the place where Jesus died.

It is difficult to realize that Jesus came to fulfill the scriptures, but He did. The book of Isaiah tells of the coming of the Messiah, or Jesus. The New Testament is filled with the life and actions of Jesus. The Gospel of Mark and Luke tell us about Jesus preaching, teaching, healing, and delivering. With Jesus dying on the cross for us, we were given the privilege of receiving our healing.

Chapter 4: The Power of Words

<u>Third Heart Attack and Triple Bypass Surgery</u>

It was November of 1994, and my husband had a new duty station at Fort Gordon, Georgia. My full-time job was volunteer work. I was still working vigorously on large, church-based projects. I was establishing relationships with community leaders and local government to set up programs for the needy. I worked for a ministry and didn't get paid. I covered my own expenses and never asked the church for money. I wanted to provide clothing and food for the needy, especially children, and to provide book bags and school supplies.

A few days before Thanksgiving, I started having chest pains and numbness in my arms. I went to the Emergency Room for evaluation and was quickly admitted. The blood test indicated I was having another heart attack!

I continued to deal with pain and discomfort from heart palpitations. The first familiar sign of a real problem was pressure in my chest and pain radiating down my left arm. I was feeling ashamed that I had allowed myself to be in this position again. The worst feeling was the wait to be admitted. My mind kept fluctuating from being a believer, to doubting that I was going to be healed. I was in a danger zone, physically and spiritually.

Each trip to the hospital I wondered, "Is this going to be my last time?" As time went on, the situation continued to get worse. I was under the care of Dr. Neasman again at Eisenhower Medical Center. My husband asked him about the prognosis and Dr. Neasman gave me less than a year to live. The stent he'd placed in my heart before was not working anymore, and I was going downhill very fast. I started laughing after I was given my death sentence. I *refused* to let that report get into my spirit. I boldly said, "God determines when I die, not man." They sent in a social worker to judge if I was mentally stable, but I knew what news not to accept. Psalm 118:17 kept ringing in my mind and Spirit: "I shall not die, but live and declare the works of the Lord."

By this time you may be wondering, what caused all of my heart problems? I missed all of the signs. (1) Pain that would not cease upon resting. (2) Pain radiating through the arm. (3) Nausea and sweating. (4) Breathing and digestive issues. It was stress, lack of exercise and improper diet, and a bad HDL (high cholesterol). I was impacted by having a family history of heart disease and did not make the right choices concerning my own personal health. I was too involved in the welfare of others. The official diagnosis was Coronary Artery Disease.

While waiting in the CATH Lab, I kept going in and out of consciousness. The only way for me to survive was to have bypass surgery, and I had very little chance of surviving. The doctor planned on rerouting the blood around the clotted artery. This procedure is called a coronary artery bypass graft surgery, or CABAG. Three vessels were blocked with plaque. My first heart attack was so massive; it destroyed my left arteries. This surgery required several veins to be taken from my right leg, leaving an incision from the thigh to the ankle. Three veins were grafted into my heart. This procedure is called triple bypass surgery.

I requested that the doctors put together a "saved" team of believers. I went directly into surgery on Thanksgiving Day. In the operation room, the bright lights and the cold equipment startled me. I remember being on a cold table and requesting several blankets to stay warm. My eyes scoped the room, and I could see the nurses gathering large needles and scalpels. A nurse began to mop my chest with betadine solution and draped a curtain over my face, I was frightened and felt alone. Everyone in the room was busy doing what they needed to do to prepare. No one was talking to me. Simultaneously, a nurse on the left side began to add sedation medication to my IV while the nurse on the right side connected the blood pressure cup. All I could think about at this time was, *What if I die? No! I will not die!*

Waking up in the recovery room, I heard the nurse call my name. The song "His Eye Is on the Sparrow" was playing ever so faintly from the attendant's desk. I focused on the lyrics, which said that God takes care of the little sparrow (bird) and I know that He will take care of me. I found myself being filled with emotions, and the tears just flowed. It was overwhelming to know that I had survived again. I had an encounter with God. In that moment, I asked for an anointing to survive the ordeal and to carry out my destiny. It was at this time that I knew what I was destined to do. I know why my life was spared. Clarity.

The kids came to visit me while in the recovery room. They said my color was like an elephant; I was gray all over and I was hooked up to lots of intimidating machinery. Vincent Jr., my oldest son, said it was hard on him to see me like this. He saw me as a powerful woman, yet there I was, connected to so many tubes and wires. My movements were slow and heavy. He had been told that the operation was a success but the recovering patient in front of him looked like a stranger. There was a feeling of death in the room. Even though the room was well lit, it still felt dark and gloomy.

In one of the lighter moments, my two sons noticed that every time I would breath, one of the machines would move up and down. They found it fascinating and kept asking me to take a deep breath. Again, they saw me on the road to recovery. They too knew that I had escaped death once more. I had been on 100% oxygen for several months prior to the surgery. My house was full of large and small tanks; I also had a portable device. Nights were the worst time, I had to rest in a recliner because I would get congested in the night and it would become hard to breath.

Recovery from Open Heart Surgery

I survived the open-heart surgery, and my recovery went quickly. The daily pain was very intense, though. Every time I coughed, the pain would radiate throughout my body. My sternum was cracked open during the surgery for access to my heart. They gave me a red, heart-shaped pillow to contain the painful vibrations of the coughing. Any kind of movement was extremely painful on top of the pressure in my chest from the wires. Regardless, I was thrilled that I could breathe without oxygen tanks! It was no longer painful for me to take a deep breath. It is a strange feeling trying to catch your breath. The lungs are struggling.

In the days ahead, there was pain in my diaphragm and in my leg. There was a five-inch cut on my leg. It was difficult to do every day routines.

It was excruciating to adjust the pillow to sit up. I really had to become dependent on pain-relieving drugs. There was great consideration before I made the decision to take the drugs. I did not want to come out of my circumstance with a drug dependency, but I experienced discomfort and misery daily and my mind would race in all different directions. I even contemplated if I wanted to live or die. Why should I have this long, slow death when there were so many other people I knew who had died immediately? I thought about my children and my husband living without me. I just wanted to give up because of the pain. *How can I make my death look like an accident?* I wondered. I wanted the family to receive double indemnity from the insurance company.

Thoughts of death and despair began to enter my mind again. I began to mutter what last preparations needed to be made. I wanted to set the agenda for my funeral. I had made up in my mind to have a home-going celebration. I knew the songs I wanted sung and which minister would perform my eulogy. For many days, I allowed my mind to ponder my death. It seemed like a better option than the pain I was experiencing, along with my nagging feelings of depression and discouragement. My mood was forever fluctuating.

Then I listened to a taped sermon entitled "Who Is Talking?" by Dr. Sandra Kennedy, my pastor at Whole Life Ministries. Listening to that sermon, I realized that each day before a person awakes, someone or something will determine what kind of day he or she is going to have –negatively or positively. I began to get an idea that someone was talking to me negatively in the morning, even before I woke up. Throughout the day, I kept listening to those negative thoughts. By the time the evening came, I was more depressed than ever. As the night set in, my sadness and depression grew worse.

From Pastor Kennedy's teachings, I surmised that from the time you get up until the time you lie down at night, someone is talking to you. That someone could be the Spirit of God or the Devil. What you begin the day with will set your mental state for the rest of day. You can agonize over what the Devil says or rejoice over what the Spirit of God says. Call those things forth.

I created my own environment with my words. If you speak defeat, then defeat is what you will get. If you make positive confessions, you will eventually obtain success. This especially applies to dealing with a traumatic situation.

Do not speak defeat over yourself. You have the ability within yourself to call things as they are.

Get into agreement with the Word. Otherwise, you are allowing thoughts to control your mind and speaking them over you. The Word of God is a change agent. He responds to His Word.

What do you do when your body is telling you how it is feeling and showing you signs and symptoms? It is not just positive thinking, but confessing, saying what God says about the situation.

It is difficult to speak the Word if you do not know the Word. The Scripture says in Isaiah 55:11, "So shall my word be that goeth forth out of my mouth, it shall not return unto me void, but shall accomplish that which I please, and it shall prosper in the things whereto I sent is." The Word of God will accomplish what "I" say and believe. You will call those things as Jesus sees them. He said in His Word that, "You are healed." In the same vein, Romans 10:9 states, "That is thou shalt confess with thy mouth The Lord Jesus and shalt believe in thine heart that God has raised him from the dead, thou shalt be saved." The Hebrew word for saved is *sozo*, which means "healed, delivered and set free." So if I am feeling sick, it is important to speak what God says about my condition.

Sickness is not from God; it is from the pit of hell. God is not trying to teach you anything when you feel pain. From your suffering you may learn many things about God, but He is not the orchestrator of your suffering. Many times people cause problems in their lives by (1) not following God's physical laws (putting on weight by not eating properly); (2) not forgiving; (3) unbelief; and (4) negative confessions. Sickness and disease are the result, and they are not in your life to stay unless you have given them room to grow. Satan will give you a symptom, and you will spend more time talking about the symptom than confessing the Word over it. Before you know it, it has manifested itself.

We cannot waiver in what we are confessing; we cannot afford to switch back and forth in what we truly believe to be true. Whatever is happening, it is subject to change. Let's look at the story of Abraham and Sarah. Genesis 17:2: "A covenant was made between Abraham and God." Genesis 17:19: "A promise that the seed will come through Sarah his wife." Hebrews 11:8-11: "By Faith Abraham believed that he would be the Father of many Nations, only because the Lord has made him a promise."

How could this happen when Sarah, his wife, was barren and both of them were beyond the age to conceive. I am certain that every time he repeated what God had promised, the people laughed at him. Even Abraham laughed at what God said in Genesis 17:17: "By faith Abraham had traveled to a new country based solely on what God stated." And in Hebrew 11: 8-11, "Abraham somehow knew and trusted God to bring those things to pass."

Abraham used his mouth to change the situation by believing and speaking the *Word*. Every miracle in the Bible resulted in a changed situation. The idea of prophecy is subject to change. Everything is subject to change; the only thing that will not change is your faith. Your faith is what propels you to believe and trust.

For the first six weeks after my open-heart surgery, I needed a lot of help; primarily, because my husband was retiring from the military at the same time. After 20 years of service in the army, he was adapting to the civilian workforce and his sometimes 24-hour workday of being a physician. It was a stressful time for our family.

Vincent Jr. realized that it was up to him to be the man of the house while his dad was gone. Victor was younger and not expected to understand everything. The man of the house role was something Vincent Jr. took very seriously. Even with my son's help, I still needed someone to help me with my daily hygiene routine. I was physically unable to do anything. The Lord sent a beautiful lady named Juanita. She was a lady that I had met at church. We warmed up to each other and she knew of my condition. She came to stay with me during the day and helped me with my routine. I was relieved to take a shower, or to simply roll over.

I remained emotionally out of control, however. I was still bouncing around with doubt. I wondered why I was still alive. Why did I survive a massive heart attack the first time? I had a friend who died from a heart attack and I wanted to know from God why I did not die. He simply told me that it was not my time. I had more work to do!

The worst pain during my recovery was in the leg where they removed the vein to put in my heart. There was a large gash that extended the full length of my leg, from the ankle to the mid-thigh area.

Vincent Jr. and Victor attended middle school during the day, but they had to care for me during the evening until their Dad got home. It was a lot of responsibility for Vincent Jr. But with no other family in the area, we were doing our best to make everything work. He even had to illegally drive the car on occasion to pick up items I needed from the local store. He was only 14 at the time, but he was an excellent driver.

The kids were so concerned that I was going to die. They felt as if they had to guard over me at all times.

Over the next year, I participated in cardiac rehabilitation three times a week. I would finish the walking and slight aerobics and receive certificates for each one. I tried to reduce my stress level, but sooner or later I returned back to my old habits with too much church work and too many stressors.

The Word Is Seed

The Word of God is like a seed. (Luke 8:11) The farmer has a crop to plant, but he begins with one seed that is planted with the expectation it will produce fruit. Let's look at Matthew 13:23 for an example: "But he that received seed into the good ground is he that heareth the Word, and understandeth it; which also beareth fruit and bringeth forth some an hundredfold, some sixty, some thirty." I have to hear the Word and get a good understanding of how it can transform my life. I have to move from positive thinking to faith. Faith is believing it before you see it.

Also, look at Mark 4:14-20:

The sower soweth the word. And these are they by the way side, where the word is sown; but when they have heard, Satan cometh immediately, and taketh away the word that was sown in their hearts. And these are they likewise which are sown on stony ground; who, when they have heard the word, immediately receive it with gladness; And have no root in themselves, and so endure but for a time; afterward, when affliction or persecution ariseth for the word's sake immediately they are offended. And these are they which sown among thorns; such as hear the word, and the cares of this world, and the deceitfulness of riches, and the lusts of other things entering in, choke the word, and it becometh unfruitful. And these are they which sown on good ground; such as hear the word, and receive it, and bring forth fruit, some thirtyfold, some sixty, and some an hundred.

This is the parable of the growing seed. The example is like that of a farmer planting crops. The farmer can place the seed on various kinds of soil. There is the stony soil, where nothing can penetrate. The reference is likened unto people who hear the Word of God given to them and they received the Word (or seed) gladly, but they do nothing with the seed. The seed falls on the type of ground (or person) where nothing is able to penetrate it. There are no roots growing, no extension to the "life-giving" soil planted underneath the surface. They can only endure for a short time. When afflictions (sickness, illness, disease) and persecution come, they are not prepared. Many of us sit in churches or listen to CDs, or even tune in to spiritual programs on the Internet, but how much of the Word of God becomes information only?

For so many years, this was me. I knew all of the Bible stories and could quote many Scriptures, but the Word of God never settled in my Spirit. I was satisfied with knowing the Bible stories and a few Scriptures about prosperity. I was an excellent teacher of the Word of God. I raised my sons to respect the Word of God, and I taught them the Scriptures. As time went on and my health worsened, I felt the need to discover what the Word of God was all about. As I faced more and more physical and emotional problems, I needed to be prepared to fight the good fight of faith.

Let's examine the second type of soil. The seed is planted among thorns. This is like planting your seed among weeds and expecting a harvest. The harvest of the Word is the expectancy, to think that something will happen or that things can to be turned around. Among thorns, there are things that prevent the seed from maturing. These things are called the "cares of this World." We can be so concerned with living that we have no time to read and digest the seed (the Word of God). We are striving to make more money and to achieve many *things*. Do not get me wrong here. I am not saying that you should not pursue richness or better living. I am saying that if you apply the scripture from Matthew 6:33, you will discover that the first thing that God wants us to do is to seek Him. To seek first His kingdom and then His righteousness means to turn to God for help. When you are "seeking" something, it means to search out and to discover.

According to the Greek Hebrew definition, to seek first is to "place in order of importance, firstly, at the beginning." So what are you seeking?

I was not seeking righteousness at first. More than anything I was concerned about making money. I was not concerned about the kingdom and God's daily principles. I wanted to just live my life.

Here's more about the Kingdom of God. <u>Righteousness</u> means "majestic, gloriously, be risen triumph." God wants us to look to Him first for help. He wants us to believe His Word, to fill our thoughts with His desires, to take on His character for your pattern and to serve and obey Him. *In everything*, He wants us to live in victory over our circumstance and trials. He has given us the method and format for what He calls success.

So the cares of this world - the deceitfulness of riches and the lust of other things entering in - chokes the Word of God and it becomes unfruitful.

The third, and last type of soil is where the seed is sown on good ground. These are those that hear the Word of God and allow it to penetrate to their soul-ish area. They hear it, then receive it and as a result bring forth fruit.

To receive the Word is "to accept, to admit." I had to accept the fact that I did not have it all together. I was not able to receive what the Word could do for me. Mainly, because I did not know what the word said. Healing is a gift from God, and it is part of the atonement of Jesus Christ. I had to accept that fact.

The third soil is called "good ground." It is at this point that the seed will flourish. It has been planted on fertile soil; therefore, yielding a product.

105

The other type of soil cannot yield anything. It is covered by weeds and stones, blocking the seed from reaching the soil.

The seed not only needs a rich soil to be planted in, but it needs the sun to help it to grow and the roots to make it stick. Likened unto the Word of God to feed our souls, the Holy Spirit to come alongside and teach us; we then will produce like seed. There will be many times that you must seek God to pluck up the weeds in your life, be it past attitudes and hurts, rejection, abandonment, and other issues that weigh us down. Yes, it may take some time before the fruit is there, but know that God is working underneath it all.

Your Word Is Seed

With your voice, you can talk to your body. Often people speak negatively to their bodies without even knowing it. When you make inadvertent remarks such as: "They just get on my nerves," or "My head hurts," or "Every time I see them my blood pressure rises," or "My aching back," or "I'm coming down with something." Just like a farmer who plants a seed and expects a harvest, we plant seeds with our words.

Your spoken words are giving instructions to your body and your body will begin to respond to what you have said. The Bible is clear about how the tongue can be used to harm or to improve your existence: "The tongue is a fire…." It can corrupt the entire body. (James 3:6) It was important that I control what I was speaking about the situation. The Bible says, "a man's belly shall be satisfied with the

107

fruit of his mouth; and with the increase of his lips shall be filled." The valuable part of these verses is that life and death are in the power of the tongue. I can control my destiny by speaking what the Lord says about the situation.

It is not always easy to speak forth the Word; it takes a conscientious effort to think about what you are saying. It has to be a deliberate act. Did you know that your words could affect your immune system? You can speak sickness and illness in your life. Your words must be chosen words. They can be a blessing or a curse. It all depends on you.

"Whoso keepeth his mouth and his tongue keepeth his soul from troubles" (Proverbs 21:23)

You should call forth your healing. Speak positively and say what the Word of God says about your condition. This is more than positive thinking. Repeating God's Word and affirmative speaking are two different things. Does what you are saying lineup with the Bible? Unfortunately, I did not understand all of this. I did not understand the importance of saying things out loud. I did not understand the importance of me saying what God says repeatedly over my circumstances. If I had known what to do, I would not have suffered as much.

In John 10:10, the Bible called the enemy a "thief." He comes to *steal*, *kill*, and *destroy*, but Jesus came that they may have life, and they might have it abundantly. Satan will keep you from embracing God's Word and having abundant life.

Satan wants to steal the Word of God from your mind. If you are grounded in the Word, you will not waiver or be discouraged by misleading physical symptoms. Satan wants to first get you so confused that you are not able to fight. He first tries to attack your memory. Satan is the author of confusion.

Whenever you have difficulties getting your thoughts together, know that it is of Satan. The Word of God says in 2 Timothy 1:7 "For God has not given us the spirit of fear, but of power, and of love and of a **sound mind**."

Hebrew 4:12: "For the Word of God is quick, and powerful, and sharper than any two edged sword, piercing even to dividing asunder of soul and spirit, and of the joints and marrow, and is a discerner of the thoughts and intents of the heart."

I had to spend time meditating on the Word of God. I began by accepting the fact the God loves me. I came to realize that the Devil is a liar. He does not reveal the whole lie at one time. It is his intent that you believe the lie to be truth or he will present only part of the truth. My head was crowded with thoughts of neglect, abandonment, fear and self-pity. I doubted myself and did not trust the people around me, especially Church folks. In my past, they had consistently failed me.

The enemy will also steal the Word of God from your memory, and if you cannot remember the Scripture, then you cannot use it. We do not want to admit that Satan is the one who is trying to steal our memory. Many of us will say it is due to our age. I knew the Word of God from Sunday school, however medications aided Satan in his attempt to rob me of the Word coming forth from *my* lips.

Satan knows that we, as Christians, will confess the Word for a little while, but as time goes on we begin to waiver. Satan is aware that if a trial lasts a long time, you will often not stay consistent in your belief. This is more than just recalling the Scripture. It means getting it down in your spirit.   The enemy will try and use your past sins against you. The Word of God says in Isaiah 43:25: "I, even I, am he that blotteth out thy transgressions for mine own sake, and will not remember thy sins."

God had chosen to forget our past.

We must also, choose to remember God's Word. In Proverbs 4:20-22 it says, "Attend to my words, incline thine ear unto my sayings. Let them not depart from thine heart. For they are life unto those that find them and health to all their flesh." I had to *say it!*

Taking Control of Your Thoughts

Your thought process is just as important as your confessions. Proverbs 23:7 says, "For as he thinketh in his heart, so is he...." What kinds of things occupy your mind during the day? This is important to consider because your thoughts have creative powers. Get your thinking in line with God's Word. A negative thought process leads to a negative mind, and a negative mind produces negative results. As you think, so you are.

Matthew 12:33: "Either make the tree (your thoughts) good, and its fruit good; or else make the tree (your thoughts) corrupt, and his fruit corrupt: for the tree is known by his fruit."

Let's look at our lives in correlation to this Scripture. The Bible says that "a tree is known by the fruit it bears." We can look at the disposition of a rude and mean person and know what kind of thoughts he has had. The fruit of this person is that of rudeness. The same is true for a kind and gentle person. Their reflection shows kindness and gentleness. Your thoughts will determine your fruit.

The Bible says in James 1:8 that "a double-minded man is unstable in all his ways. A double minded man (a man that cannot make up his mind) wavers back and forth between his carnal mind (not born again) and his spiritual mind."

To get control of my thoughts, I had to get control of my emotions. This was the biggest problem I had to face. We, as human beings, have been given the ability to reason and create thought patterns. Our thought patterns are greatly influenced by our morals and values. Where did you first have impressions about certain things? We do not always know why we feel the way we do because emotions have always been an area that we do not fully understand. The Bible refers to that part as "the hidden person of the heart." (1 Peter 3:4). Scholars call him The Holy Spirit.

Have you ever felt that the person you present to the world seems different than the person on the inside? Or vice versa? I did! I felt as if there was a war going on within me. This is because there is one part of us (the inner man) that wants to do right and the other part (outer man) that wants to do wrong. We are confronted with making decisions daily. We often get bombarded by negative thoughts and lose our way.

My life had been drastically altered by my illness, and my emotions were everywhere. One minute I was sad, and the next minute I was happy. One minute I had high hopes and the next I was completely down about the situation. I had to learn to control my emotions better.

If you find yourself in a negative area and feeling emotionally down, ask God why you are feeling that way. You may be surprised when He gives you the answer.

When I would see myself heading down a dead-end road that would lead to depression and hopelessness, I somehow knew that I had to flip the situation around. The first step was for me to make a decision to look at things differently. If I made the right decision, my emotions would eventually follow in line. The key is to make a decision *immediately!*

As situations arise and we are waiting for a miracle from God, we really must deal with our emotions right then. Problems will not take a rest. They keep on coming.

The second step is to believe that things can change. God will give you strength to overcome the situation. Philippians 4:13 says, "I can do all things through Christ who strengtheneth me." It is at this point that you have to put Scriptures that will speak positively in your life. It is the Word of God that will heal. The Word of God is like a two-edged sword that will go forth slaying whatever is in the way of your healing. I spent time reading and meditating on the

Word of God while in His presence, and I received the strength I needed.

During your periods of frustration, the Devil will try to invade your thoughts and convince you that your faith is not working. Situations would play over and over in my mind like a broken movie projector. I had to remember that Satan is a liar and a deceiver. If we respond to situations the way God would, our trials can become easier. On the other hand, if we complain and show resentment, our trials will become harder. I had to make up my mind to go beyond positive thinking, but to apply my faith. Faith believes before you see it. Faith is believing God's Word. My body screamed out loud daily. Aches and pains were a part of my daily life. I did not want to become addicted to prescription drugs for pain. I allowed my mind to take over and say that I was not in pain.

I have a great deal of respect for people who I know are going through trials and put forth more than a positive attitude. It is not necessary to discuss ailments and every doctor's report. Accept the facts and know that God is bigger than the facts. It is important here to speak positively. No, I am not saying that you do not have that particular problem or ailment, but every comment you make does not have to be negative. Remember, you are prophesying over yourself. Once I realized that life and death were in the power of my tongue, I recited this prayer to give me strength:

> "Dear Heavenly Father, I shall
> not worry about anything but
> in everything I will pray with
> thanksgiving. I will let my
> request be made unto You, Oh
> God. I will let the peace of my
> God which passeth all my
> understanding to keep my

heart and mind through Christ
Jesus." Philippians 4:6-7

Hindrances to Your Healing

We all have things in our lives that prevent us
from receiving the full benefits of our salvation.
Based on the Bible, here are some of the common
hindrances to our healing:

(1) Lack of knowledge

This is not knowing what the Word is saying
about a situation or being unfamiliar with the
Scriptures. The Holy Spirit will begin to move upon
you when He finds favor in what you are doing. If you
do exactly what the Bible says to do, the Holy Spirit
will encourage you because you are basing your
actions and attitude on the Scriptures. Many people
have been taught differently about healing. God does

not go by what you are taught, but he goes according to what He has said in the Bible.

(2) Not Forgiving

This is an unwillingness to forgive other people for wounding you or harboring old feelings, which produce bitterness and anger. Always remember that forgiveness is a decision, not an emotion. *You* are the one that has to make the decision to forgive. This includes forgiving yourself. This was a tough area for me. I struggled, with bouncing emotions, from not forgiving others and myself.

Matthew 6:12: "And forgive us our debts, as we forgive our debtors." If you forgive men when they sin against you, your Heavenly Father will also forgive you. But if you do not forgive men their sins, your Father will not forgive your sins. This is according to Matthew 6:14-15: "For if you forgive others their trespasses, your heavenly Father will also forgive you, but if you do not forgive others their trespasses, neither will your Father forgive your trespasses." There is another Scripture in Mark 11:25-26 that says "And when ye stand praying, forgive, if ye have ought against any; that your Father also which is in heaven may forgive you your trespasses. But if ye do not forgive, neither will your Father which is in heaven forgive your trespasses." The Scriptures makes this point very clearly.

During the course of living life, you will face the decision to forget and forgive. I had become angry with my family members and members of the church. This was much of my problem. I had issues in my life that were crippling me from year to year. At one point I realized that the anger was killing me more both mentally and physically. I was losing sleep just staying up and replaying the "memory tape." After months and months of rehearsing the emotional trauma over and over, I could see that it was affecting my health.

I would spend nights wondering why I had not dealt with it a different way. I would have nightmares and night sweats, tossing and turning. The enemy only presented the negative. It was my responsibility to take control of my thoughts. The Bible says for us to think on things that are true, whatsoever things are honest, whatsoever things are just, whatsoever things are pure, whatsoever things are lovely, whatsoever things are of good report think of those things. (Philippians 4:8) I would think about the ocean and the calming effect of the tide and waves coming in and out. I would remember the seagulls landing on the waves. My mind would focus on the beautiful sky that radiated God's awesomeness and His creation. I would think about the blooming petals of a rose. I would think about a wonderfully made newborn baby coming into this world with awesomeness. I would marvel at the squirrels running about freely in the rustling of the trees. I had to lasso my thoughts.

I knew that if I had held on to those feelings "my" health would be affected. The other person(s) were going on with their lives. They had no idea of the offense. I wanted to fight everyone, and in doing so I sent my immediate family in torment. My children had no way of knowing which Sarah would show up from day to day. There was the angry Sarah that yelled at any little thing. Their rooms had to be spotless. They had to respond swiftly if I called their names. My husband probably suffered the most as he tried to provide love and attention. Times around me were rough.

Others saw me as kind, friendly, and receptive, which was far from the person that lived inside of me. We would plan family outings and I would ruin everything by excessively disciplining the kids. I also tried to satisfy my emotions by shopping. My actions would kill the monthly budget and prevent us from becoming debt free. I would buy and buy just to receive immediate gratification. All along I was playing the church wife, mother, and minister. I presented myself as if I had everything under control. I was far from it, but I knew all the church expressions to keep people away. I was a hard shell to crack. It was easy for me to display the "well put together" Sarah, from head to toe — I was sharp. Through therapy I learned how to unravel the layers. The first step was to acknowledge my shortcomings.

I will never forget what my, then 13-year-old, son said in a family meeting. He said that I was confusing him. He went on to explain that no matter what I told him to do, he was going to receive punishment. If he made the bed for example, it wasn't made right to my standards. He would wait to take the beating because I would discipline anyway. I had to be in control. During therapy, I came to realize that I was doing just what my mother had done to me. Behavior patterns were repeating themselves. After making my lists of disappointments and frustrations, it was discovered that the results, positively or negatively, were ultimately my responsibility. It was really hard to love me. I would not let anyone inside my heart. Bitterness had set in.

According to Hebrews 12:15, bitterness is a root. The tree's roots are buried deeply under the ground, and we see the results above the ground. Bitterness will hide itself deep within and cause you to erupt for any reason. The purpose of a root is to manifest on the surface, but to brew under the surface and to fuel things. It was difficult for me to see that bitterness was hiding within me. It was a deadly poison that needed to come to the light and be addressed in order to bring myself out of a state of spiritual and emotional unrest.

As an example of my inability to forgive, I had another close friend and we shared everything together. We were spiritual sisters. One day I had a dream and I shared it with her. It was concerning the Church and actions that were going on there. The next Sunday, the Pastor preached about the exact same thing we had talked about. I made the bold assumption that she had discussed it with him. The situation put a wedge between us. I exploded! I left a message on her answering machine not to ever call me again or to approach my children. It was a nasty message. It hurt her as much as it hurt me. I was not sensitive at all. Years later, I discovered that she did not discuss it, but it was the work of the Holy Ghost.

The Holy Ghost had touched the pastor's heart and he was responding to what the Lord had said.

It was the work of the Holy Ghost that I did not understand. The Holy Ghost is our teacher and our revealer. I asked my friend and God for forgiveness. I needed to ask for forgiveness and to receive forgiveness. My friend and I made up, and we love each other; we are still together as best friends. But things are not the same. Jesus tells us to be sensitive to other people needs, even in little things. I was wrong not to take heed.

I am glad, though, that I was able to make peace with my mother before she passed away. The Lord even used me to lead her assuredly to Christ. Reconciliation with her was the hardest thing I have ever done, but it was the most rewarding.

(3) Unbelief

Simply not believing that the Word of God is true is called unbelief (as opposed to disbelief). Rebuke the devil and he will flee. In Mark 9:23 Jesus said, "All things are possible to him that believeth."

Hebrews 11:1 says, "Faith is the substance of things hoped for, the evidence of things not seen." "Boldly confess what you are believing for, and God will work on your behalf." (2 Chron. 6:9) "He will give you everything you ask Him for." (John 15:7) Talk as if you have it, and it will come. If you are speaking words of doubt nothing will happen for you. If I had confessed words of doubt, then nothing would have manifested in my life. Nothing positive, anyway.

I needed the kind of faith that Abraham demonstrated after receiving a promise from God that through Sarah he will be the Father of many nations. This was especially profound, since both of them were beyond childbearing years. How can an old lady and older man conceive a child? Certainly each time he made the confession, people laughed at him. However, his confession stayed the same. He did not waver based on the promise of God. I could not waver. I had to confess it just to possess it!

God only asked me to believe that it was already done. My natural eyes could not see this; I had to use my spiritual vision. What did the Word of God say about the situation? I found the solution in the Scriptures.

(4) Pride

A prideful, haughty attitude will block the healing power of God. (Proverbs 16:18) I was basically unteachable. I thought I knew it all. Nothing could make me change my mind. I floated on a haughty image.

I felt that I could convince others that I was right and everyone else was wrong. I could tell them what they needed to improve or to do. Proverbs 16:5 tells us that that kind of domineering, superior approach is not pleasing to God. He wants His children to walk in kindness and humility, not in arrogance and pride.

Proud people are usually rigid, which explains why I was such a strict disciplinarian. I had my own way of doing things and I wanted everyone else to do it my way...or no way!   I was a very complicated person to approach. There was no telling how I would respond. I wanted to have everything figured out and to know the "ins" and "out" of every situations. I wanted to be in control! If I took on a project, I had to be the team leader, or else. I have a special gift of organizing and getting people to rally behind projects. There is a good and bad side of this gift. I can work with other people... sometimes. Other times, I like to work solo to get more done. I have an inward desire to do an excellent job that does not always include others. To put it simply, I felt that I had to be in control because deep down inside I felt that nobody could handle things as well as I could.

(5) Unconfessed Sin

This is an unwillingness to confess your sins before God. James 5:16 says, "Confess your faults one to another, and pray one for another, that ye may be healed."

(6) Negative Confessions

Say the same thing that God says about you. What does God's Word say?

Begin to say what God says and confess that, even if your body is telling you something else. Do not confess the negative things. You will get what you say – good or bad.

Ignorance of the written Word and the inability to confess the right things brought about lots of distress. *I knew the stories* but not the application of the Word. Flippant words and expressions often fell from my lips without my full awareness of the consequences. Thank God that there are preachers out there now who teach about making positive confessions from the Word. One of my greatest desires is to preach and teach the Scriptures.

(7) Involvement in the Occult

This means involvement with Ouija boards, psychics, tarot cards, séances, horoscopes, and crystal balls. Denounce the power that these things may have over you.

(8) Laziness

This is being too lazy to look up the Scriptures and spend time in the Word of the Lord. You have to put forth the effort to obtain the provisions and promises of God.

(9) Waiting on physical evidence before you believe you are healed.

God's power to heal flows like God's power to save. You must believe.

We may not always understand why life can be so difficult. Why are children abused? Why does my loved one have to die? Our suffering does not please God, but when we have a good attitude while waiting for God to bring balance and justice in our lives, he makes the waiting time more bearable. We do not understand why children die and why our husbands and wives are unfaithful, yet we must realize that God is faithful. We may not understand why there is poverty and homelessness, natural disasters, and many other injustices. One thing I'm sure of is that

God loves us and he is able to deliver us out of any situation.

"Many are the afflictions of the righteous but the Lord delivered him out of them **ALL.**" (Psalm 34:19)

Chapter 5: The Three D's and Their Relatives

Second Open Heart Surgery

The second open-heart surgery occurred in 2011, nearly 20 years after the first open-heart surgery. By this time, Dr. Neasman had transitioned out of the military into private practice in Texas. I was now under the care of Dr. Michael Odle, Eisenhower Medical Center Fort Gordon, GA. He did research relevant to my heart condition. He discovered that Emory University Hospital and St. Joseph Hospital, both in Atlanta, Georgia, were performing heart surgeries that involved a way to reconstruct the ventricular valve of the heart and suction air into the chambers. This method is called Left Ventricular Assistance Device (LVAD), a mechanical circulatory support system.

I was given a referral to St. Joseph's Hospital in Atlanta to see Dr. Donald Jensen. He evaluated me and referred me to the heart transplant team. I was hospitalized and received extensive evaluation. It was a whirlwind of events after the first admission. There were many tests to see if I would make a good candidate for the machine.

The most amusing evaluation was from the gynecologist. It was 6:30 a.m. and she walked into the room and introduced herself. She began to complete a gynecological exam in the room with a bedpan! I couldn't stop laughing. In all my 50+ years, I have never had a "drive-by" pap smear. She was gone in minutes. I must have laughed for over an hour.

I was evaluated by every department, from endocrinology, hematology, dental, eyes and every other part of the body, along with the Social Worker to determine my readiness. They had to make sure that I had support at home. From these evaluations, the heart transplant team had to make a decision about my candidacy for a heart transplant.

Periodically, during my 10-day stay at St. Joseph Hospital in Atlanta, Dr. Jeffery Miller would come in and out of the room. I knew that he was my surgeon, but I had no concept of what that really meant or the importance that this man would later play in my life. Within two weeks in the hospital, my whole life changed. The team members would come by daily to reassure me about the surgery. As the night of the surgery grew near, more and more fear tried to enter my thoughts. My bed became as hard as a rock and the room spun around constantly. Somewhere between consciousness and unconsciousness, I knew that something was about to happen — something that would change my life.

The day before the LVAD surgery a new nurse came into the room. I was captivated by his warm smile. He introduced himself as the LVAD (Left Ventricular Assist Device) nurse that would assist in the surgery. I was not certain of his role, but his soothing voice and confidence gave me much needed assurance. Still, fear wanted to enter my spirit. Tears began to form in my eyes. It was hard to hold back the fear of the unknown that kept creeping up my back.

Nurse Alisha assisted in the operating room. She reassured me that all would be well. Each sentence I tried to make was more and more difficult to get out. The medication was beginning to affect my body.

My body began to tremble and my thoughts became cloudy.

The anesthesiologist mumbled something to me. It was urgent for me to calm myself down. *Get control of yourself Sarah*, I thought. I knew that becoming emotional would shoot my blood pressure out of control and maybe cause a stroke. The management of my blood pressure was in my control at this point. As a person who likes to be in control, I was frustrated because I had no control of what was going on in the room. I had to trust and rely on their expertise. I constantly prayed that they would be very alert and at their best.

The room around me was full of large, intimidating equipment. The lights were blinding and the odors were foreign to me. I heard plastic tearing. In periods of consciousness, before the surgery began, I could finally see the suture kits and knives that the doctors were going to use. My mind wandered upon Scriptures that I learned in my childhood. I wondered what would be the outcome. Fear, once again, tried to capture me. I continued to feel it rising up. *Lord, what will be the outcome? Will I survive the surgery? Could I trust the doctors? I cannot back off now. I will stand on the scriptures.* **I am healed.**

They put a taped curtain around my face, and then I began to panic. Again, the nearby technicians reassured me. "Calm down, Mrs. Ferguson. Calm down," they said.

The anesthesiologist gave the consent for more medication. I was strapped to an operating table. As the medicine entered my body, I felt like a prisoner waiting to receive the final dose of something lethal.

Will it kill me? Will I come out paralyzed or in the form of a vegetable? I wondered.

One Scripture stayed in my thoughts: "I shall NOT die but live." (Psalm 118:17) Was this a statement of desperation or merely a statement of declaration? I could not recall the rest of that Scripture. My mind kept wandering. *What is the rest of that Scripture? Lord, I want to remember. Lord, will you hear just part of it and recognize it?* I was not sure, but I started to pray: *Help me, Lord Jesus. You know it is my heart's desire to see my grandchildren thriving as young adults. Lord, don't let me have a stroke. Will I wake up with all of my faculties in order? Will my worst nightmare come to pass? Will my children be looking at me in a nursing home from a comatose state? No, I will not accept any of those lies. I am healed!*

It seemed like I had been asleep for only a few minutes. The sounds in the room became clearer. I heard the beeping of the machine, the startling alarms and tinkling of bells.

What was happening? Why was the nurse
yelling at me?

"What do you mean, calm down? I am calm!" I
tried to answer, but I could not say a word.

My thoughts ranged from the hospital arena to
beautiful sounds on the beach. One minute I was
watching the seagulls and the next minute I was lying
flat on a cold table.

Voices from the distance drew me to the
present. *Where am I? Who are those people? Get that
bright light off of me!*

I was afraid and I laid there feeling puzzled. I
thought, *Lord, I cannot do this in my own strength; I
will not walk in fear.* I could not get my thoughts
together enough to remember where that Scripture
was in the Bible. Suddenly, I remembered it was in
Deuteronomy 31:6: "Be strong and of good courage,

fear not, nor be afraid of them; for the Lord thy God, he will not fail thee, nor forsake thee."

In the Critical Care Unit, the bells kept ringing on the monitors. I quickly looked over at my blood pressure and I could see that it was rising. I could not physically point to it and tell it to calm down, but I mentally told it to calm down. The siren stopped. I could recall looking over to my right and there was another person lying so still in the bed. I began to question why I couldn't lie still. I tried to place one foot on the floor thinking, *I need to get up; I need to get up*.

The nurse asked where I was going. I needed more sedation.

A cool breeze became present in the room. My thoughts went back to the sounds of the beach and became clearer with each moment. My mind traveled back and forth. I felt another cool breeze and I was surrounding by large feathers. Then there appeared two large beings. They never spoke a word, but they kept moving their wings. This motion generated a cool, calm, and tranquil feeling within me.

My thoughts went back to the hospital room. *Where is that voice coming from?* I could not identify it. More voices. *What are they saying?*

"Lower her head," a nurse said gently.

The feathers began to move back and forth, and a cool breeze continued to fill the room. I looked up to see if it was the air conditioning, but it was the motion of the feathers moving the air. I realized that these were my angels surrounding my bed. I knew it was them because of the peace I felt. I could not see their form or their features, but I felt the gentle breeze surrounding me. They were the prettiest feathers I had ever seen in my life. Bright colors – red, yellow, blue, green, just like the colors in the rainbow. It was

144

contrary to the traditional depiction of angels we see here on earth. It was awesome and beautiful!

As I continued to drift in and out of consciousness, the breeze soon left me. I immediately began to have a feeling of calmness and peace like never before. The quietness in my spirit lowered my blood pressure. I knew that I had been in the presence of the Lord and His angels.

Time flew by like it was seconds. When I woke up, the nurse was calling my name. As I tried to talk, she said, "Wait till I remove this trachea tube from your throat. Hold your breath."

There was a gagging and a choking feeling in my throat. I could hardly hear myself speak.

Shortly after, my family entered my room. All I thought about was how intimidating it was for them to see all the equipment around me.

Three nights later, I was informed that I had been through two surgeries because the bleeding would not stop the first time. The second surgery was to close up the incision. I could see the frightened look on my sister's face at hearing this news. I knew that something had happened, but still I was going in and out of consciousness. I could not figure out what was happening to me. I wanted to sleep. I wanted to say, "Don't touch any part of my body because it hurts. Please don't touch any part of my body."

In a conversation with Ruth, another of my spiritual sisters, I began to explain the breeze that I felt from the angels. We both wept. She explained to me that the night before while in prayer she was reassured that I was going to be all right because two angels told her so. We marveled at the fact that the Lord would give so much confirmation that everything was going to be okay with me.

Hours passed and I was resting in the recovery room when a young man entered the room with a deep voice. It was an unfamiliar voice, but I could hear the authority and confidence in it. "Are you Mrs. Ferguson?" the man asked.

I nodded.

"Do you have two sons?"

I said, "Yes."

"Did they attend Morehouse?"

Again, I said, "Yes."

He said, "I have been to your house several times."

I was still puzzled as to why this young man would have visited my home

There was an awkward pause then he told me that my sons were his fraternity brothers from Alpha Phi Alpha. He said that I had fed him many times at my house. Indeed, that was true.

I chuckled and asked his name.

"Mario," he said. "I am here to reconnect your defibrillator."

We both started laughing as tears rose up in my eyes because I knew about divine appointment. He said he was not even supposed to be on schedule that night, but when he got his routine assignment, he began to wonder if the Mrs. Ferguson on his list was a person that he knew. We both were astonished to find out that we knew each other. He had finished his calibration. He reconnected my defibrillation device and in five minutes he was gone. He was there for a short while, but the moment seemed like hours.

This time around, my recovery was different. There was support from my church family. They showed up with cards, letters, and meals – everything my family and I needed. During the second open-heart, Vincent Jr. was living in New York and Victor was living in Atlanta. I am thankful for everyone who was there during my darkest moments. In the midst of the storm, I was able to find joy in knowing that God had people out there that truly cared.

Dealing with Depression

The recovery stages of all my major surgeries were often the hardest times. I celebrated the fact that I was alive, but it was a sensitive process. When I concentrated on the negative, it led me down a spiral path to self-destruction. I found myself in a dark hole of depression and heading to suicide. Before I knew it, I was there – somehow caught up on the road to a nervous breakdown. To help prevent that, I kept a journal to write down my thoughts, feeling, hopes and dreams for the future. Writing helped me to see myself outside of the struggle. I had to set immediate goals and make plans to live. It was a choice that I had to make, in order to stay focused on fulfilling my goals. I wrote about friends and loved ones. Very few people knew that I was depressed because I was able to hide it publically. Negative thoughts would enter when I was alone.

Suicidal thoughts can be managed. Learn to recognize the subtle warning signs from your body. As you learn to manage your episodes, you can avoid highs and lows. Contact a friend or family member and let them be warned about your behavior. You should watch and list the warning signs in your journal. If the high and low feelings persist, consult a physician. There could be a chemical imbalance you're unaware of. You should also avoid any alcohol intake during this time.

I found myself having wild mood swings and outbursts. I was swinging between feeling positive, and feeling like I was in total disparity. It was at this point that I would wonder what would happen if I stopped taking my heart medicine? Would my heart stop? During those times, I felt ready to see my Maker. I needed to make up in my mind if I wanted to live or die. I had to fight! The Bible says in 1 Timothy 6:12 to "fight the good fight of faith…." I had to roll up my sleeves and **fight.**

Keep in mind that some medications may cause these problems. This is why you should follow the instructions and guidance of a doctor. The problem for me was staying focused on the desire to live. I had to live one day at a time, no…one hour at a time!

There was the constant bombardment of doctor's reports. I had to make a choice. Of course, I could not believe the doctor's report. With each report came more depression. Do I believe everything that was said? Do I believe the lab reports? Surely, they are facts. I have to put God above all of the reports.

In my mind, I was still physically healthy. I could not get my mind around what was happening to my body. I had to believe that there was someone in charge of my life that was higher than my understanding. My faith had to be activated to believe and stand on the Word. A state of hopelessness floated above my head. People who are depressed often experience the following:

(1) Hopelessness or helplessness

(2) Rapid gain or loss of weight

(3) Appear listless and even complain of feeling "down" or depressed

(4) Divorce, loss of job, long-term illness, legal troubles, and financial difficulties.

There is always a root cause for depression. Disappointments will lead you down a path of depression. When we expect certain things to turn out a certain way, and it does not, we become disappointed. When dealing with expectations from others, they can let us down; we become disappointed. We are also disappointed when we expect certain things from ourselves and feel as if we let ourselves down. That feeling of letting yourself down can lead to shame. You may not want to interact with others and you may even feel as if you do not deserve to be on this earth. Any form of actively wishing your own death should be dealt with immediately!

Out of control emotions can wear you down to the point that you become tired and sick. Having anger, feeling guilty, having wandering thoughts and frustration can make you tired. I had many anger issues. Issues with family members, church members, church leadership, and my health contributed to my physical condition. I hated the fact that I was sick and I felt guilty about how I got to that point. I also had difficulty asking for help. My emotions were definitely out of control. My family did not know how to treat me. I was gentle one moment and radically taking their heads off the next. Since my husband is a doctor, he immediately recommended I get help. Of course, I did not pay him any attention! I had a breaking point where I would do nothing but cry all day. I felt wounded and rejected.

Thoughts of defeat continued to drain me. It was fear that was manifested through my emotions. Our emotions will lead us to doubt and have simple unbelief. This is not pleasing to God. Our thoughts can lead us to distrust people, especially when there are old pains that have not been dealt with.

I did not know how to search the Scriptures to find what I needed for my situation. In a sermon, I heard the message that God did not want me to perish because of a "lack of knowledge." As a result, I sought help from a psychiatrist. It was through many hours of therapy that I finally dealt with church issues and the need for approval from others. Thank God for the treatment of my psychiatrist and medications that helped to balance my emotions. There were days when I could hardly get out of the bed. I would hide myself under the covers and refuse to talk. I would not answer the phone or receive guests. I remember once, a new friend named Sandy Jenke came over to my house and insisted that I get up from under the covers. She took my head in her hand and said to me, "Your grandkids need you." What she said was a little funny because neither of my sons were married nor had any children. She was prophesying my future. She was letting me know that I *had* a future. It was an in-your-face encounter! After hours of crying, praying, anointing, reading and crying some more, she left me in a much better state of mind.

Thank God for friends like Ruth, Mildred, Sandy, and Sandra who kept me in their prayers. They travailed before the Lord in fasting and in prayer. The Bible talks about four friends, who let the roof off of a building to get their paralyzed friend to see Jesus and get his healing. (Luke 5:18-20) They were not only foolish to cut the roof on the building, but their faith was so strong that they knew if they put their friend near Jesus, he would be healed. It took faith and strategy for that miracle to happen. Thank God for four foolish friends who believed in hope when there was no hope. Thank God I was willing to change because I was truly heading down the road of self-destruction.

Dealing with **D**isappointment

There were times that things seemed so overwhelming for me. I was disappointed in so many things. Many of my disappointments that I had to deal with involved the church and my family. I could not understand many of their methods for doing things. I was disappointed in the friends who turned their backs on me when I needed them the most. I had been a friend to them during their illnesses and the deaths of their loved ones. Yet, during my illness, they never offered to do one thing for my family. It seemed like some friends conveniently forgot where I lived. This was confusing and frustrating to me. The golden rule is to treat people like you want to be treated. I had to stop the blame game. It had been so easy to blame others like my mother, my children, my spouse, and the church people. I had to learn to forgive and move on. I was shaken by disappointments, I had to break through and find inner strength. After lots of therapy, I came to the realization that I cannot change a person, and I am not responsible for another person's decisions. I used part of the Serenity Prayer as my prayer of focus:

> God grant me the serenity to accept the things I cannot change, courage to change the things I can, and wisdom to know the difference. Living one day at a time and enjoying one moment at a time.

Dealing with Discouragement

Church Relationships

I had to learn how to forgive others and move on. This was an enormous task. My soul side (mind, will and emotions) wanted to strike back; however my spiritual side knew that this was important for my spiritual growth and development. The harboring of that negative feeling supplemented my confusion and despair. Forgiveness was my next course of action. When you harbor ill thoughts about others like I did, it only affects you. This discord caused me physical and mental pain. It also damages new relationships and the way you view others. Always remember: Forgiveness is not for the other person; it is for you.

Forgiveness will help you to move forward and to stop looking back. I had spent far too many years dealing with unforgiving thoughts about people and situations. There is no doubt that to look back and reflect on your mistakes from time to time is a good idea. However, it is not a good idea to continue to play that record repeatedly. What has happened has already happened! Dwelling on missed opportunities or replaying conversations will not bring it back again. Thinking about what went wrong and why it went wrong leads to being "inactive" and wanting to give up and give in. I realized that my negative thoughts affected and harmed me in many unconscious ways.

It is important to develop a new attitude about possibilities. My new attitude required action. But as you know, it was not easy to say or do. Words like "think positive" or "just forget about it" or "everything will be fine" or "cheer up" are useless unless you have the correct perspective on the situation. Thinking about a mistake of the past can unleash dozens of negative thoughts. There were times that I could not stop the negative them. I had to renew my mind. I had to plug in what the Word of God says about the situation and how it could affect me positively. When thoughts of disappointment came into my mind, I had to learn not to exaggerate them. Those exaggerations only made me feel worse.

I had an all or nothing approach to everything, as well as being a perfectionist. If I did not perform perfectly, I would feel embarrassed, disgraced, and doomed about the situation. I lived in woulda, coulda, and shoulda-ville. I thought that if I was not given the opportunity to preach or teach that it was the end of the world for me. Many of my conversations were simple misunderstandings, and the inability to express what I really wanted to do. I wanted to magnify the potential results of any mistakes.

I took the time early on to write down the mistakes that haunted me. My therapist instructed me to write down my thoughts about my mistakes, missed opportunities, and injustices. I did this project for several months before I got a revelation. It is important not to just say things in your mind, but to commit it to paper. When I was able to visually map out my insecurities, it brought healing to me. At one point I felt like a failure when I began to question whether or not I was a good mother, teacher, or preacher. It seemed as if nothing I did turned out well. I listened to comments about me from naysayers. Why could I not fit in? Why does my mind seemingly race ahead of others? I felt troubled and doubted people around me. For someone that succeeded most of the time, I felt like a failure. I was screaming on the inside because nothing I said mattered to anyone. The lies kept flowing. Church people kept gossiping.

After dealing with the dissolutions from people in the church, I did not want to have anything to do with the church or any of the people who attended the church. A deep depression had taken hold of my life, and I was ready to give up on both people and life. I felt as if no one cared about me. I felt as if they only wanted what I could do for them.

I came to seriously realize who my real friends were. I only mentioned friends because we lived far away from any of our family members.

I had fallen prey to all of the three Ds – depression, disappointment, and discouragement. I had little will to live and I did not care if I woke up the next morning. I was sick of being sick, and tired of suffering only to *exist* each day. Many days I would leave the curtains pulled, not answer the phone, and refuse to get up and even put on clothes.

Being a Parent, Wife, and Family Member

I also had a problem with bitterness, anger, and not forgiving others. Those are a lot of problems, but not too overwhelming for Jesus. The days had to be filled with Scripture reading and meditation. The emotional healing took place as I acknowledged it. That was *huge*. By confessing my shortcomings, I gave Jesus something to work with. Certainly each problem had to be dealt with individually and it took a lot of time. I do not want to wax over this lightly because it is a continuous process. The enemy will bring the situation up again and again. I was truly mean to my children; nothing they did would satisfy me. I had very high standards for them. I trusted very few people and allowed my sons to interact with very few people. My youngest son wrote me a painful letter where he questioned why I did not trust him to make the right decisions. He had ventured out beyond his curfew and was harshly punished for it. I continued to remind him of the incident and held it over his head each time he asked to go out. He questioned why I was so mean and so distrusting. My battle with church members affected my ability to trust my son and his friends. Somehow I had to get over that issue. Here are a few of the affirmation statements I used to help me. I used Scriptures and affirmative statements like:

> I am strong.

> I have a good attitude.

> My thoughts are positive.

> I am redeemed.

> I am forgiven.

> I have the favor of God.

> I have a sound mind and etc.

Additionally, I made declarations about whom God is:

> He is the supreme God.

> He is mighty.

> He loves me and cares for me.

> He is my peace and joy.

> His mercies are new each morning.

> He is my healer.

I still make these confessions with the Scriptures throughout the day. (These daily confessions, including the Scriptures, can be found in my *Daily Deliverance* book).

I had a vision of seeing myself out of the situation. A vision is the desire to move ahead. I would have stayed stuck in yesterday without a new vision for my life. The Scripture says, "Where there is no vision, the people perish..." (Prov. 29:18) The Devil wants you to live in yesterday. He is the one that is always reminding you of the past. I could not receive what God wanted for my life by constantly thinking about my past.

One day I found a Scripture for my newly transformed life. I had experienced ministers teaching about forgiveness, but one day that Scripture pierced my soul (mind, will, and emotions).

Matthew 6:14-15 says, "For if you forgive other people when they sin against you, your heavenly Father will also forgive you." I made a change! The side effects of that change have given me a longer life and a more peaceful spirit. Contrarily, if you do not forgive men their sins, your Father will not forgive your sins.

The second Scripture that became a Rhema Word (meaning a word that reached deep down within and was transforming for me) was Matthew 7:3: "Why do you look at the speck of sawdust in your brother's eye and pay no attention to the plank in your own eye."

Many times I had heard messages on the topic of forgiveness and judging but I remained extremely judgmental. I would look at a situation and make my own deductions and reasoning without even getting to know a person. I would comment about the attitude of people without knowing about the circumstances in their lives. I placed myself on a righteous pedestal and became an ungodly judge of others. I had to realize that unless I brought my faults to the surface, it was impossible for God to deal with it. I have witnessed that if you live openly and go down a clearer path of confronting your true self, flaws included, change will be a lot easier. You are a contributing factor in both your physical and spiritual healing.

It is our mandate to live a good life here on earth; a life that will lead people to Christ. However, this is impossible unless you make an effort to improve your sinful nature. God wants to empty you out and fill you with *His* precepts and nature. I felt bound for heaven, but I was leading a poor Christian life here on earth because of my behavior and attitude. I spoke the Word, taught the Word and preached the Word, but my life was a poor example of the impact of the Word. Thank God I had found the answer! Once I learned to forgive, it became easier to move on from my past. This was not an easy process simply because I had real reasons to be angry with people. More than anything, I thought I could control people and situations.

My negative emotions caused me to be reluctant to receive the love from people in my life, because it led me to judge and not trust.

Chapter 6: Victory Is in Believing

The Battle Is in the Mind

There is a battle going on in your mind. Ephesian 6:12 says, "For we are not wrestling with flesh and blood, but against principalities against powers, against the rulers of the darkness of this world, against spiritual wickedness in high places."

We have to make up in our mind that we want to believe in what the Scripture says about a situation. We can stay in the past and wallow in our self-pity. On the other hand, we can get up and live victoriously, knowing that the blood of Jesus has already cleansed us.

Paul says that he "will forget the things of the past and reach forward to the things ahead." (Philippians 3:13) God will forget your past, and He will allow you to use the experience to glorify Him and to encourage others by your testimony.

For example, some people are in physical bondage from Satan. They have ailments and conditions that plague them constantly. The question here is whether or not they are embracing the ailment. Many Christians embrace their sickness and are fooled by Satan into thinking that sickness makes them more like Jesus. I never received this! I refused to embrace anything. Somewhere in my childhood I was given the foundation to believe in the Bible. I knew that Jesus went about the earth healing and delivering people. I knew all of the Bible stories and believed that they were true. I knew that suffering was not God's plan for us. The more I learned about Jesus, the more I began to understand what was won for me at Calvary. I was not going to embrace the negative. Contrary to that thinking is the fact that

"Jesus came to heal," and "The thief cometh not, but for to steal and to kill, and to destroy; I come that they might have life, and that they might have it abundantly." (John 10:10) Yes, the enemy is trying to kill you with sickness, disease, and turmoil.

Certainly Satan did not want me to have a successful marriage. He tried to bring discord and strife into my marriage. Before Vincent and I were married, we would have violent arguments and subsequently separated. This time, we had severed our relationship and we were trying to move on. One day I was outside of his home in Columbus, Georgia and we had a very serious argument. I had parked my car at the bottom of the hill and had begun to walk toward it when a car came around the corner and violently hit my car, knocking it into a tree. It was a hit and run. We looked at each other and simultaneously said, "*God is trying to tell us something,"* we decided to get married. From that point on we agreed not to violently approach each other. Later in my life, violent behavior would creep in as I would discipline the kids and in my interactions with others.

One of the ways Satan works is by trying to get you to forget God's Word. He can attack your memory as well as claim your mind. You can combat this by first realizing that you have the mind of Christ. Corinthians 2:16 states, "For who hath known the mind of the Lord, and he may instruct him? *But we have the mind of Christ."* I had to speak and declare this daily over my life. You need to meditate on God's Word. When you put God's Word in your spirit, the Holy Spirit will bring it forth at the time of your need. To combat the loss of my memory or the ability to recall Scriptures, I needed to meditate. Meditation is an ancient art that has been abused and misused.

The man who meditates upon the Word will be prosperous and successful in all that he does. Meditation firmly plants and instills deep roots in a man. As I meditated on His Word, I found that God removed unbelief from my spirit.

Speak to Yourself; the Creative Power of Words

Ephesians 5:19 states, "Speaking to yourself in psalms, hymns and spiritual songs, singing and making melody in your heart to the Lord." In doing so, it will strengthen your inner man Since the beginning of the world, words have been in existence. When God made us, He gave us the ability to speak reason and to think for ourselves. No other life form on earth has this ability. God spoke when He created the world. Genesis 1:3 states, "Let there be light." Immediately, light appeared at His spoken Word. This was a simple expression of what was to happen.

Many other times in the first chapter of Genesis God spoke and things happened. V6: "He spoke and created the firmament." V11: "Let the earth bring forth grass...." V20: "God said let the waters bring forth abundantly...." The words "HE SAID" appears ten times in the first chapter of Genesis emphasizing the importance of the spoken word.

You have that same creative power in your tongue. By releasing your faith, the creative power will bring God's Word to pass. When God spoke, power was released and things began to move. Even man was created in Genesis 1:26 by the spoken Word of God. In Genesis 1:28, God blessed Adam after he spoke it forth. In Genesis 1:26, He created Adam in His own image and in his likeness. In Genesis 8:28, God blessed Adam and said unto him, "Be fruitful and multiply, and replenish the earth, and subdue it: and to have dominion over the fish of the sea, and over the fowl of the air, and over every living thing that moveth upon the earth." God gave man the power to rule and have dominion over this earth.

Just as God created the world with His tongue, you have creative power for healing. I mention in Chapter 4 that **YOU** can speak to your body and tell it with authority what to do. You did not have to worry about destruction and even death, until Satan's fall from heaven. Satan even referred to himself as a god. Isaiah 14:13- 14 states, "I will ascend above the heights of the clouds; I will be like the most High." Satan wanted to stand equal to or above God. This broke the spiritual law and violated the limits of his authority. God's Word reined victoriously over the word of any angelic power.

In the third chapter of Genesis, we can see how the enemy took God's Word and tried to deceive Adam and Eve. 1 Timothy 2:14 states, "Adam was not deceived but the woman being deceived was in the transgression." Adam knew that he was disobeying God's command. It is through this disobedience Satan was able to obtain authority on earth. However, you must remember that God is more powerful than Satan. Jesus defeated him. God sent His Word and healed them. Isaiah 55:11 states, "So shall my word be that goeth forth out of my mouth; it shall not return unto me void, but shall accomplish that which I please, and it shall prosper in the things whereto I sent it."

I found the pattern for my prayers in Mark 11:23. In summary, it says that I can say to my mountain (problems) "be removed and cast into the sea." If I do not doubt in my heart but shall believe that those things, which I have said, will come to pass. I can have whatever "I SAY."

But Satan will try to plant a seed of doubt. He will ring out such comments, as "If God will heal, then why hasn't he?" He will try and plant doubt in your mind. He will offer words and suggestions that God is not God. Slam the door on his lies and suggestions. I do not know why God choses to perform miracles in one life and another person will die suddenly. I will not even attempt to explain this, however, we do not know what their real confessions have been. Perhaps they have uttered to the Lord that they are tired. God will not override our will.

Creating the Right Seed

When I was going through hardships and things seemed impossible, it was good to remember the Word of God that was planted in my heart. It is at these times that it seems impossible to read and comprehend the Word. I spent many days just trying to live on my own strength. However, as I travel along this life journey, I am reminded of the Word of God that was planted in my heart as a youth. The Word of God tells me to "attend to his words, incline thine ear unto my sayings. Let them not depart from thine eyes; keep them in the midst of thine heart. For they are life unto those who find them, and health to all of their flesh." (Proverbs 4:20-21) This is a clear instruction for me to listen.

I discovered another point; if I blessed others, I will in turn be blessed. Take a minute to be one with your words. Your comment maybe the only positive thing they have heard today. You are planting a seed. I soon discovered that there is a boomerang effect here. You will get back what you need. When I moved beyond myself, I began to see results in my life. Your greatest test is when you are able to bless someone else while you are going through your own storms in life. I not only felt good about helping others, I stopped focusing in on myself. In addition, my heart felt grateful that I was able to do something for someone else.

What happens to a person who is fed negative suggestions by a mother, father, or even a sibling? Your subconscious is almost forced to be influenced by such negativity. Mine was. It has to be a way of life to put away the negative comments and responses. If I spend time complaining about my problem, I will be over powered with difficulties. To get myself out of trouble depends upon what "I SAY." If I confess sickness or poverty that is exactly what I will get. I was constantly discussing what the Devil had done to me. I made the enemy bigger than my God. When I became aware of what I was saying all the time, I wanted to change. No one corrected my confessions! I started to correct myself. I had to make God bigger than my problems. It was only after I started

confessing the Word of God did I notice a turn around.

Change does not occur overnight, it is a slow process.

The healing process began on the inside and later

manifested on the outside. Daily I felt better and

better. I found strength to do the things that had

interested me again.

It was a slow process, in view of the fact that I had

numerous years stating the problem. Do not replay

the problem, talk about the solution. See

yourself healed and set free. I had to become my

own cheerleader.

It is my responsibility to get deeper meaning

and understanding about what the Bible has to say

about health and healing, in order to grow stronger in

my Christian faith. I am the one who controls what is

tuned into my spiritual ears and what I keep in my

heart. It is my responsibility to protect my mind and heart from the enemy. The Bible says in John 10:10 that Satan comes to kill, steal, and destroy.

Also, Matthew 4:15 states, "Satan comes immediately, and takes away the Word that was sown in their hearts." This is the reason I had difficulty remembering specific Scriptures. The Word of God is our fighting source. It is the only ammunition that will destroy the works of the enemy. Romans 10:8 states, "The Word of God is near me, even in my mouth, and in my heart." I had to say what I believed.

This too shall pass; trouble did not come to stay. It must yield to the Word of God and the blood of Jesus.

III John 1: 2: Beloved, I wish above all things that thou may prosper and be in good health, even as thy soul prosper." God wants me to prosper and to be in good health. Can you ward off Satan with your ideology? No, he will destroy you. Again, the only weapon that is effective is the Word of God. Hebrew 4:10 states, "For the Word of God is quick, and powerful, and sharper than any two edged sword, piercing even to the dividing asunder of soul and spirit, and the joints and marrow, and it is a discerner of the thoughts and intents of the heart." The Word of God will penetrate cancer, and pull it up from the root. The Word of God will create a new physical heart. I had to embellish the Word of God, and to make it a part of my life.

To keep the enemy from stealing the Word when he attacked my memory. I would hear a sermon or listen to a tape and would not remember one single thing. I came up with the idea of writing down the Scripture on 3x5 notecards. I concentrated on the exact Scriptures that I needed for my situation.

The same can be done to protect your memory. Every time I would try to study the Word of God, I would become confused as to where to find the passages. I used the index that was available in the back of my Bible to locate the passages. Once I found a scripture that met my need, I would record it and put in all over the house. Every time I looked in the mirror, I saw Psalm 118:17: "I shall not die by live and give God the glory."

Negative confessions will yield only negative results. Romans 10:9 states, "If I confess with my mouth and believe in my heart that God hath raised him (Jesus) from the dead, thou shalt be saved (healed, delivered and set free)." This scripture can apply to every sickness and disease known and unknown to man. It can also apply to substance abuse and deliverance from satanic influences. If we confess our sins, and believe in our heart, God will

184

bring it to pass. Romans 10:17 states, "Faith comes by hearing, and hearing by the Word of God."

I am sure by now you want to scream and shout, "I have done all of these things, but nothing seems to change!" Remember that healing begins on the inside. Continue to apply what the Word of God says. A farmer keeps watering, and fertilizing, and watering and fertilizing with the expectation of receiving a crop. There are scriptures that I confess several times each day. Psalm 118: 8: "It is better to trust in the Lord than to put confidence in man." And Psalm 118:17: "I shall live and not die and declare the (glorious) works of the Lord."

When I have doctor appointments, I repeat these Scriptures. I refuse to let negative thoughts enter my heart. Yes, the doctors are speaking the facts about my condition, but the Word of God is the final word.

Finding Your Focus

The biggest and strongest enemy in your life is
your thought process. At a young age, when a boxer
usually starts fighting, he has the self-confidence to
win. With training and preparation, he would win a
few and lose a few fights. As he begins to move up in
weight and class, his opponents get stronger, faster,
and quicker. This is the same way with our spiritual
walk with God. When we are first born again,
accepting Jesus Christ into our hearts, we know
nothing about the Word of God or anything about the
power of God. As new beginners, we have to start
reading the Bible to find Scriptures and grow in the
Word. I had to learn to *believe* God was able to fulfill
his Word. I was not just going after healing, but
instead I was walking as if I was already healed.
Though my body cried otherwise, I had to go beyond

hope. I needed to step out on what I knew was true: the Word of God.

The Lord paid the price on Calvary. Your first encounter maybe something as small as a headache. If you apply the Scriptures on healing, speak to your body, and demand that the headache leave your body, there will be victory. You can apply the Scriptures to cancer, heart disease, diabetes or any other ailments that would come your way. You can be trained and tested by reading and believing in the *Word*. You can prove that God Himself is a healer. More importantly, you will know for yourself that He is the Healer.

What kind of things are you focusing on? What sort of thoughts guide your day? Are you talking more about the problem by saying, "My aching back" or "My heart attack" or "My sugar" (diabetes)? First of all, that claims each of those illnesses as yours.

Just by saying the word "my," you take ownership of the problem and make it an everyday part of your life. Then what should I say? You should say what God says about the situation. Acknowledge the human facts of the report, but understand that they are just "human facts." You say to yourself, "Whose report am I going to believe?" Find a healing Scripture, take a stand and do not change your position. God is faithful. You can declare Psalm 34:4, "I sought the Lord, and He heard me, and delivered my from all of my fears."

Another Scripture that enabled me to get through my situations was Proverb 3:5-6: "Trust in the Lord with all thine heart; and lean not unto thine own understanding. In all thy ways acknowledge him, He shall direct thy paths." Biblical Scriptures like this provide insight into how people should live their lives.

The book of Proverbs teaches one how to attain wisdom. It is a book that requires discipline around what is right or wrong. To lean on the Lord means to put all of your trust in Him (His Word). It involves actions as well as attitude. To lean infers to putting your whole weight on something. Resting and trusting in a person or thing. God gives us the ability to reason, but we cannot trust our own ideas because our minds will wander and convince us differently. There are times that you do not know what to do, so it is wise to seek spiritual counsel. However, be aware that this could be a trap of the enemy to keep you in the same position to lean on peoples' thoughts and ideas. Make sure they are using the Word of God as their base for information. Your healing begins on the inside. Speak to your body and command it to work.

It is also important to walk in faith without being foolish. The doctors will confirm healing in your body, but continue to take the medicine prescribed in the meantime. And pray over all your medications. You should pray that there will be no side effects. Remember, the medication will dowhat it is designed to do. Be completely compliant to the doctor's instructions. There will be sudden changes in your body, which can be easily identified and verified by your physician.

How to Get Your Thoughts Under Control

In order to get your thought-life under control, you first have to get your feelings and emotions under control. Your thought-life is fed by your emotions because it is what you feel and think. There is always a war going on inside of our heads. One part of us wants to do what is right and the other part wants to do what is wrong. It is confusing; the wrong things can feel right; and the right things can feel wrong. We

190

make excuses for our decisions because our feelings often vary and are unreliable. We may choose to do the wrong thing simply because it seems right at the time. You can battle with your thoughts and emotions to a point that it becomes a relentless struggle.

It was a constant battle for me to want to live and to move on from the past. Nothing seemed to work: not friends, not family, and not even church. I had lost hope, and hope is the key ingredient that leads to faith. It is the expectancy that a situation will improve and the outcome will be favorable.

Trust in the Scripture

Through trial and error, I discovered that it is not wise to request patience. For the Scripture implies that to get patience, I would get trails. Instead, I realized that patience was already given to me, and that I will identify with it. It is one of the fruits of the Spirit. This is clearly stated in James 1:2-4: "My brethren, count it all joy when you fall into divers temptations; knowing this, that the trying of your faith worketh patience. But let patience have her perfect work, that ye may be perfect and entire, wanting nothing." Romans 5:3: "...and the fruit of the Spirit is love, joy, peace, longsuffering, gentleness, goodness, faith, meekness and self-control." Certainly, I was experiencing a trail and I began to examine what was coming out of my mouth. I would cry and scream to the Lord, *why?*

I got my answer; it was in the words that I spoke. Crying and balling did not move the Lord instead he was compassionate. He began to speak to me about what I was saying. A previously typical conversation would begin with a narrative about what was going on in my body. I had to describe visibly what was going on with me. I would list the problems and complained that I was getting tired. One day, I so clearly heard God say, "*listen to what you have just said.*"

Your mouth is the waterspout for producing what you have called forth in your life. Your mouth determines your crop. It takes faith for you to believe that you have patience when nothing within you seems to possess it. You have to know that patience is working in your life even when you do not see it. All that I felt and thought could change. The Devil uses the same tools to get you to believe the lying symptoms. He will stop doing what he is doing to you when you stop responding to what he is doing. It takes faith to activate what God has put inside of you. You should stop talking about the problem, call those things as though they were, and speak the positive, according to Romans 4:17.

Chapter 7: Starting Again

Recovery from LVAD Surgery

The purpose of the LVAD machine was to give me a better quality of life, since I was in the later stages of heart failure. My life greatly changed after its installation. I was discharged from the hospital and went to live with my youngest son, Victor, who lived in Atlanta. He was between jobs and had the time to take care of me. I had to stay close by the hospital for six weeks until I was cleared to go back to Augusta. My husband had to stay in Augusta and work. He joined us on his off days. He still had to provide financially for both households as a contract doctor. Victor had to take a crash course on how to change the bandages, how to know when and how to change the batteries, and what to do in the case of an emergency. The machinery was intimidating. Victor had to reassure me that he knew what to do. My recovery was in his hands. My chest had been cut open again and was healing. Victor said that I looked like I had turned into a cyborg. The cord of the device protruded out from the flesh of my stomach and into a hand-sized mechanism that had two heavy, Samsung Galaxy-sized batteries attached to it. At first sight, he commented, "They have rebuilt her."

"Faster and stronger," I replied.

Victor lived in midtown Atlanta in a place that was noted for housing artists and musicians. The halls were full of smoke and music was always blaring.

This was not the place for a fairly conservative evangelist like myself. Victor had to reconstruct his life around me. It was his intent to change my diet and to get me healthy. The first two weeks I spent mostly sleeping. The rest of the days were spent with the occupational therapist. When I was awake, we spent the days exploring the art side of my personality. We were writing songs, and exploring the Bible. I'm not a big fan of daytime television. It was a teaching moment for me, Victor was excited about learning about the Bible. By the third week, I was able to use my momentum to get up and move around. Daily, I grew stronger and less tired.

On my high-energy days, Victor and I would explore the neighborhood in a wheelchair. He took me once to a historical graveyard, which was about a block away. We talked about how defeat was not an option in either of our lives and the opportunity and privileges that were available to us still being above ground; how we are always capable of greatness; how we had a real encounter with life and death; and how our lives were enriched. I saw his flaws that couldn't be seen through a phone call and he saw the same.

We spent all of this time together because I could not be left alone to take care of myself. My being there was a great inconvenience for a single, young man, yet he never made me feel unwanted. Instead, he was compassionate and considerate in every way. He saw me in my worst condition, and I have never heard him complain. Instead, he admired my tenacity and my willingness to change. He accompanied me to all of my clinics and wellness treatments. He allowed me to spend time with his friends and to impart God's goodness. We both grew towards God, each other, and towards our best selves.

Facing the Odds

There was a time that my blood level got extremely low. I was fainting and felt quite weak. It turned out that my hemoglobin was at transfusion level. Over the period of a month, I received six transfusions and was admitted frequently. After many tests, it was discovered to be a small bleed in my stomach area. I had microscopic surgery and it was repaired. Each time I received a transfusion, I would pray. First, I thanked God for the blood. Second, I claimed that no bacteria shall be in the blood. Thirdly, I took authority over my body and commanded it to accept the good from the blood and reject the bad. Throughout all of this, I did the same thing with my regular medications; prayed over it first and then took it as prescribed.

I thank God for a good support system. These were the people there to stay up with me at night, to prepare food, to help give me a bath, to call and provide Scripture, or just to listen to me. One of the requirements for a heart transplant is to have a good home-based support system.

The hallmark of one of the most beautiful elements of my life is my marriage. In December of 2012, we renewed our wedding vows after 30 years. It was the rebirth of my happiness and the shedding of the dead skin of disparity and conflict. At the celebration, Bishop Larry Skinner, the minister who performed my wedding ceremony the first time was present to do it again. I was elated to also have the presence of my new pastor, Dr. Sandra Kennedy, as one of the officiants. It was an awesome and anointed celebration with family and friends.

Haunting Thoughts of Death

Death was all around me. My heart muscle was strained. I was exhausted physically and mentally. Yet, in my spirit I knew that I would make it. In my prayer time, God assured me that I had more work to do and death would not over take me. God would place friends to give me the same messages, over and over. No matter what they saw physically, they continued to stand with me and say, "I shall not die, but live and declare the works of the Lord."

No matter how many times the thought would come up, I had to keep repeating what outcome I wanted to receive. It was important that it came from my mouth. I had to go with what God had said, contrary to my mind and body. The physicians made sure that my heart rate did not get elevated or that there was no stress on the heart. This was controlled primarily with medicine.

The Enemy Thought He Had Me

I needed to conduct myself peacefully, even in the mist of circumstances that would be very traumatic. Had I not been so peaceful, the monitors would have sounded off indicating a rise in blood pressure. In order to maintain that level of peace, I had to let go of anger and strife. Strife is vigorous bitterness, quarrels, or discord.

I had to be courageous. It was a matter of digging deep within to stand the test. I had to lean and depend on God to supply my every need. Peace was my objective. Peace is a "fruit of the Spirit." The nine fruit of the Spirit are Love, Joy, Peace, Patience, Kindness, Goodness, Faithfulness, Gentleness, and self-control. The fruit of the Spirit are God's divine personality that is worked in overtime into the Christian's human spirit. (Galatians 5:22-23) The *fruits* are evidence of Godly character in our lives.

Additionally, I discovered a need to ask for strength. I could recall Ephesians 6:10: "I can do all things through Christ who strengthens me. My spirit shouted, "I am strong in the Lord and in the power of His might."

I quickly realized that I could not do it in my strength. I meditated on these Scriptures, repeating them over and over. I had to renew my mind by saying what God says about the situation. I *chose* to look through the eyes of God, and he called me whole. There is nothing lacking, nothing missing, and nothing broken. This wholeness comes from our relationship with God. He wants us to have a healed soul (mind, will, and emotion). We can have these provisions by taking it with faith.

There is a recurring message throughout the Bible; God's people do not have to be afraid of anything, because He is ultimately in control of all things. He is surely going to work it out for my own good. Romans 8:28 says, "...and we know that all things work together for good to them that love God, to them who are called according to his purpose."

Behind the scenes God is working it out, my responsibility is to not faint because of what is going on around me; but instead apply Galatians 6:9: "And be not weary in well doing; for in due season we shall reap, if we faint not." I had to get over my fears and get my anxiety under control.

I declared that it was my season, and I would not be weary in it. I would encourage myself by thinking how Great my God is and what he has already provided.

Chapter 8: God's Word is True

<u>Peace</u>

During all of this, I ended up being calm. I cannot explain why. But I can tell you how. The calmness came as a result of learning to trust God. I had been assured that it was not my time to depart this earth. How many times does God have to reassure me? I suddenly found peace. I discovered that God's peace was already planted inside of me. All I had to do was to draw it out. It was a choice. Do I stress or do I trust God?

Peace is defined as tranquility, harmony, or security. Peace is directly related to the actions and attitudes of individuals, however peace is ultimately a gift from God. Peace is tranquility of the soul. It is the ability to be calm and demonstrate inner stability.

It allows me to conduct myself peacefully, even in the midst of circumstances that would normally be very nerve-wracking, traumatic, or upsetting.

I discovered that there were a lot of things disturbing my *peace*. There were peace stealers called wrath, anger, and strife. The definition of wrath is rage, resentment, fury, violence or stern displeasure, and severe annoyance. Strife is bitterness, discord, and a quarrel. The peace that I was looking for was not of the world, but the peace that is defined in John 14:27:

> Peace I leave you, my
> peace I give unto you;
> my peace I give unto
> you; not as the world
> giveth, give I unto you.
> Let not your heart
> be troubled, neither let
> it be afraid.

This peace is because of Jesus Christ.

What can I do to maintain my *peace*? I can walk in love. For example: love is never envious, nor boils over with jealousy and is not boastful. It is not conceited. It is not rude. Additionally, 1 Corinthians 13 says, "Love is kind."

When you walk in love you are patient, because love is patient. When you walk in love you are kind, because love is kind. When you walk in love you are not envious of another person, because love is not envious. When you walk in love you put yourself aside to help others, because love is not self-seeking. When you walk in love, you are not easily angered because love keeps no record of wrong.

These were tall orders for me, but it was a measuring point. The Holy Spirit convicted me; I had to repent and try not to make the same mistakes. Especially, when it came to not being easily angered. How did my love walk affect my *peace*?

>I have to be patient and kind... reduces my frustration with others.

>I cannot be jealous.

>I cannot be conceded.

>I cannot be rude... expressing what I feel all the time.

>I cannot be touchy... easy to blow up in anger.

>Does not apply blame... looks at one's self.
The bottom line is that my job is to walk in love to maintain my peace. There were so many stressors that were trying to steal my *peace*.

Church workers	Jealously
Home responsibility	Envy
Distractions	
Disruptive Conversations and many more.	

In order to deal with others and maintain your peace, you have to put aside your feelings sometimes.

This is operating in the soul-ish area (the mind, the will, and emotions). Remember, we are three-part beings. We live in a body, we are a Spirit and we have a soul. It was my emotions that triggered my acting out. I had problems with speaking out and giving my opinion. Of course, I had to be right.

Selfishness shuts the door to the love of God.

The Bible says that we must pursue peace. We must go after it. We must not repay evil with evil, but give thought to do what is honorable in the sight of God. It is up to me how much I want to pursue peace. It is my goal to live in peace with others. What changed my attitude? It was the desire to relieve myself of stress and stressors.

Romans 12:17-21 says, "'Vengeance is mine. I will repay, says the Lord." Living peacefully means leaving revenge to God and overcoming evil with good. We should be quick to hear, slow to speak, and slow to anger, according to James 1:19-20.

One of my peace stealers was jealousy. I had to stop comparing myself to other people. I had to stop worrying about myself all the time, everything was not centered on me. I had to focus on the positive in my life. Breaking free from jealousy started with me. I had to change the way I thought. It changed the way I felt and acted. The easiest way to change my focus was to begin to help others. I had to move outside of *myself*. It changed my perspective. My philosophy now is Anger, Strife, Jealousy, and Bitterness = Bondage. I refuse to live in bondage.

Another one of my peace stealers was bitterness. The Bible says that bitterness springs up like a root. Bitterness is hard to identify. It is a deadly poison. I had to go before God and seek the answer as to what was irritating and festering in me. Bitterness has a tendency to show up in anger and other negative emotions. Bitterness is like a bubbling fountain that has roots underneath and these roots will sooner or later make themselves known. A root's job is not to manifest on the surface, but to brew under the surface and fuel things. Have you ever exploded on someone for no reason? They make a simple comment and you take it to the extreme? This was me! I thought it was time to turn things around. I was going further into a deep hole.

When I was happy, it spreads. We can make people perk up and aspire to higher and better things just by our example. Your optimism can spread when you spend time with other people. We can have a real impact on others if our responses are genuine, not some kind of phony technique we come up with.

By returning good for evil I can inspire others to do likewise, instead of promoting disrespect and meanness; that only wounds others and poisons relationships. Retaliation is not the answer. It provokes others to get even more angry and ugly. Showing the right way through example and calm resolve will inspire others to react differently. We are to cultivate peace and harmony. This kind of peace did not come overnight for me. It takes practice, practice, and more practice. There will always be something or someone that will rub you the wrong way.

God is working for me, with me, and in me to fulfill His plans and purposes for my life. I can face the uncertainty of the future without apprehension and anxiety. I can do this with complete confidence, knowing that God will work all things out for my *good*.

Rest

The Lord has a lot more work for me to do here on earth. I have learned to rest in the comfort of knowing that He has it all under control. I trust God. I developed that rest after knowing that God would want me to be healthy again and to maintain a better quality of life. As I face each new day, I am aware of His destiny for me. I will live fearlessly, confidently, and worry free. Recently I celebrated my 60th birthday, 20 years after my first brush with death. I have learned to live and appreciate each new day that I am given. I will live until I am satisfied. Until God takes me safely to His Heavenly Kingdom, I will rest assured that He will give me the means to escape every attack in my life.

I became like a sponge and soaked up every book that I could find on healing and making positive confessions about deliverance. My search led me to many authors of prayer books. However, I could not find a book with short declarations that I could read daily. Therefore, I created Confessions for Tomorrow. I needed to be rescued from the pit of despair and regret. I did not know what to say to an awesome God. In these confessions I stated the problem and located a Scripture to support the solution.

I expect that at any moment the situation can change. I have to watch and wait. What do I do? Simply *believe*. We cannot quit believing. Hope is the beginning of *faith*. I had to accept in my heart that healing was for me. Jesus is no respecter of persons (Acts 10:34). What he will do for me, he will do for you. I had to believe this.

The key is to trust God!

God's highest purpose in us is to teach us how to trust Him. Trust enables God to work His miracles through us. Without *truth*, God does nothing.

Matthew 11:28-30:

> Come to me, all who are
> weary and
> burdened, and I will give
> you REST.
> Take my yoke upon you
> and learn
> from me, for I am gentle
> and humble
> in heart, and you will
> find REST for your
> souls. For my yoke is
> easy and my
> burden is light.

I choose to REST in God's Word and to trust Him, that is what gives me peace in the midst of the storm.

Restoration

The Bible says that whatever the enemy has taken from me, I can go to God and ask for restoration. This is a time of restoration. I want my stuff back. Restoration means to repay, return back, to put someone back in a prior position, and to make restitution. Joel 2:25:

> And I will restore to you
> the years that the locust
> hath eaten, the
> cankerworm, and the
> caterpillars, and the
> palmerworm, my
> great army which I sent
> among you.

I make the following declarations:

> I declare restoration of time.

> I declare restoration of my finances.

> I declare restoration of health.

> I declare restoration of family.

> I declare restoration of my peace.

> I declare restoration of my joy.

The following are declarations I make daily:

> I shall live and not die and declare the Works of the Lord!

> Praise God, His mercy endures forever.

> No matter what it looks like.

> No matter how I feel.

> I choose to *believe* that by.

> His stripes I am already healed.

Summary

We all have to go through trials and circumstances that can rock your world. Had I not be prepared spiritually, I would have died. Man said I was dying, but God said otherwise. My goal was to write this book and share with others the story of how I made it over. I was mandated to write this book. Throughout the entire book, there is a mandate that you learn to trust God. Rather you call Him God or a Higher Being, he is there to assist you as you go through your troubles.

I wanted to live a life that was worth living and to start again — this time with less anger, depression, discouragement, and disappointment. Willing to move forward, I had to take the first step toward my future.

The Scripture says, "The Lord himself goes before you and will be with you; he will never leave you nor forsake you, Do not be afraid; do not be discouraged." Removing fear was the hardest. Faith grows better when under attack. My faith is now at an unbelievable level. I had to stretch out on what the Word of God says:

> "But as it is written.
> Eyes hath not seen, nor
> ears heard, neither have
> entered into the heart of
> man, the things which
> God has prepared for
> them that love Him."
> (I Corinthians 2:9)

I believe that my *best* days are ahead of me. There is more to come. I am waiting with expectation to see what God is going to do.

I have planted a seed, now I can expect a harvest. The Lord has a lot more work for me to do here on the earth. I have learned to *rest* in the comfort of knowing that He has it all in control. *I trust God!* As I face each new day, I am aware of

God's destiny for me. I will live fearlessly, confidently, and worry-free. I have learned to live and appreciate each new day that I am given. I will live until *I am satisfied* and death does not have any hold on me! Until God takes me safely to His Heavenly Kingdom, I will *rest* assured that He will give me the means to escape every attack of the enemy. I am now equipped to fight. *Until another tomorrow!*

44468052R00125

Made in the USA
Charleston, SC
27 July 2015